How to
th

Second Edition

(formerly entitled Developing a Records
Management Programme)

Julie McLeod

and

Catherine Hare

How to Manage Records in the e-Environment

Second Edition

(formerly entitled Developing a Records Management Programme)

Julie McLeod

and

Catherine Hare

Routledge
Taylor & Francis Group

LONDON AND NEW YORK

Second Edition

Published by Routledge
Haines House
21 John Street
London WC1N 2BP
United Kingdom

Routledge is an imprint of the Taylor & Francis Group, an informa business

© Julie McLeod and Catherine Hare

Typeset in Bembo and Helvetica by
Taylor & Francis Books
Printed and bound in Great Britain by
MPG Books Ltd, Bodmin, Cornwall

Book ISBN-10 0-85142-463-5
Book ISBN-13 978-0-85142-463-7
e-Book ISBN-10 0-20340-357-6
e-Book ISBN-13 978-20340-357-0

Contents

Preface

Managing records in the e-environment is a huge and complex task. In a guide of this size we can only scratch the surface. Our aim is to provide a framework and to flesh out some of the bones for people who are new to electronic records management, in order to help them understand the issues involved and to begin to identify solutions for their own organisations.

The emphasis therefore is on

- explaining some key concepts
- outlining best practice
- indicating practical steps to adopt in individual organisations and providing
- selected resources (books, journals, listservs and relevant professional associations) to follow up, and
- a glossary of key terms.

The guide is divided into nine chapters. Chapters 1 to 3 establish general principles, which are accepted internationally, and the remaining chapters provide practical guidelines. Chapter 8 is devoted to the particular challenge of managing email. Each chapter covers a separate topic and is written to stand alone. Therefore, if the book is read from cover to cover, the reader will note that some points are reiterated. The examples, while taken from the United Kingdom, are not unique to a specific national context and therefore are applicable elsewhere.

To help individual organisations to assess and develop their approach to managing e-records, the first three chapters conclude with a list of issues to address, in the form of questions to answer. The remaining chapters have checklists to complete, which are grouped together in Appendix A.

The guide highlights a number of key principles which are fundamental to the management of records in the e-environment.

First, it is essential that items that constitute e-records are identified early to ensure that they are in fact created and captured. Secondly, the business operation to which the records relate should drive the way e-records are created and managed. And thirdly, perhaps most crucial, records carry information about and are evidence of business operations. Using these key principles this guide directs readers to the theory, so that they can understand what is involved, and to the practice, so that they can take direct action to manage records effectively and efficiently in the e-environment in the context of their own organisation.

Chapter 1

The organisational context

We live today in the information age which means that information is a key resource and exploitable asset in the home, in society at large and especially in the workplace. This is particularly true for services that add value by better, faster and cheaper information. It applies particularly in the developed world which, because of its social costs, finds it more and more difficult to compete especially in the traditional manufacturing sector.

Information comes in a variety of media but more and more is in electronic and digital format in the e-environment. This e-environment has resulted from the development of information and communication technologies (ICTs). In addition, these technologies have replaced the map of national economies and national markets with a global economy and global markets because transport and delivery costs of e-products are the same, wherever the production is happening. Competition is, therefore, worldwide.

Information is at the heart of your organisation. Much of this information will be in the form of records that your organisation generates and receives in conducting its business. In order to maintain and hopefully improve its effectiveness and efficiency your organisation must manage its information and its records. The way to do this is to put in place a framework of policies, procedures and practical guidelines so that everyone within the organisation who is involved with information and records understands and executes their roles and responsibilities in managing information and records effectively and efficiently.

However, managing information and records in this e-environment is a huge, complex and challenging task. It covers not only information in digital form, but also an environment, which, in fact, is a hybrid of paper, electronic and other formats. It involves issues at the operational, tactical and strategic levels.

This relatively short guide cannot cover all aspects of the task in detail; it can only scratch the surface. It aims to provide:

- a top level framework
- practical guidance for developing and operating effective and efficient records management for those new to managing records in the e-environment.

It also aims to:

- outline current approaches
- provide examples of best practice to help you tackle the challenges, and
- point you in the direction of more detailed information available elsewhere.

The focus is primarily on information, captured in the form of records, created electronically, but also addresses records in paper and other formats. The first three chapters establish general principles which are accepted internationally and the remaining chapters provide practical guidelines for dealing with the various tasks involved in managing records in the e-environment. The examples, while taken from the United Kingdom, are not unique to a specific national context and therefore are applicable elsewhere.

In order to establish the role and purpose of records management, we need to begin by looking at

- information and its management in the business context
- what constitutes the records of an organisation, and
- the issues relating to information and records in electronic format.

1.1. Business context and the e-environment

No matter what type of organisation you work in, you will be aware of the e-environment. In the public sector it is manifest in the e-government programme first led by the Office of the e-Envoy and which aimed, by 2005, to ensure that:

"all services which can be electronically delivered should be"
(Office of the e-Envoy, 2000)

Driven by the e-Government Unit since 2004 it has a broader mission of

"ensuring the IT supports the business transformation of Government itself so that we can provide better, more efficient public services"
(e-Government Unit www.cabinetoffice.gov.uk/
e-government/index.asp).

In the private sector a focus is e-business, or e-commerce, where the transactions between supplier and customer are contracted and conducted remotely. There are many other examples, including e-learning, e-working, e-skills, e-books, e-journals.

All of these activities use technology but fundamentally rely on information. Information is an essential input to and output from business activities. It is bought, transformed and sold, represents a corporate resource and asset and so needs to be managed. However, before focusing on information itself, we need to look at the drivers for information and records management, which will vary from sector to sector.

1.2. Drivers for information and records management

All organisations should manage their own information for business needs, i.e. to ensure the effective and efficient running of their operations. From the private sector Michael Clarke of PricewaterhouseCoopers LLP (Clarke, 2003) emphasizes this point in stating that

> "effective information management is now critical to delivering e-enabled business models required today."

From the public sector The National Archives (formerly the Public Record Office) (The National Archives, 2001) confirm that

> "information age government is underpinned by the effective management of electronic records."

So, across all sectors the importance of information and managing it effectively is seen not only as a way of doing business *efficiently*, but also as a means of doing business *better than your competitors do*. In the private sector this might mean

- getting more quickly to market with a new product
- faster turnaround of orders, and
- more flexible customer relations.

In the public sector, where the aim is to provide better customer service to the citizen, the focus will be on

- demonstrating accountability
- transparency of operations, and
- value for money.

All of these objectives depend on having to hand the right information of the right quality.

In addition to and deriving from this universal need for effective information and records management there are other drivers, which are to do with legislative requirements. Some are common to all organisations. Other legal or regulatory

4

demands are specific to certain sectors. For example, in the public sector currently, a key legal driver is the Freedom of Information Act 2000, which covers more than 70,000 public bodies in England and Wales. Issued under the Act is a Code of Practice for records management (Department for Constitutional Affairs, 2002). The Information Commissioner, Richard Thomas, declared, at the Records Management Society of Great Britain's annual conference in Leeds in April 2003 that organisations should be aiming to have well kept records to which they are happy to give access. These legal frameworks are identified and covered more fully in Chapter 4.

Other shared drivers relate to risk management and business continuity, which we explore in more detail in Chapter 5. However, there are compliance drivers, which are specific to particular sectors because of the nature of their activities. One is compliance with standards-based requirements.

Some organisations, in both the public and private sectors, are registered for compliance with such series of international standards as

- ISO 9000 (2000) for quality management and
- ISO 14001 (2004) for environmental management systems.

Both explicitly require registered organisations to create and keep records. For example, ISO 14001 (2004) specifies requirements for an environmental management system. It explicitly states in paragraph 4.5.4 that

> "The organization shall establish and maintain records as necessary to demonstrate conformity to the requirements of its environmental management system and of this International Standard, and the results achieved.
>
> The organization shall establish, implement and maintain a procedure(s) for the identification, storage, protection, retrieval, retention and disposal of records.

Records shall be and remain legible, identifiable and traceable."

Even if your organisation does not operate in a sector regulated by a specific international standard, the standards-based approach can help all organisations. David Best (BIP 0025:1, 2002) clearly identifies the general benefits of establishing a common approach, which ensures a system that is

"auditable independently of the organisational setting in which it is practised."

These general benefits include:

- consistency
- best practice, and
- the accumulation of a body of knowledge.

Best's comments relate to another standard, which is of critical importance to records management. Launched in 2001, ISO 15489 is the first ever international standard on records management. While it is not a compliance standard, the standard itself (ISO 15489-1, 2001) and the accompanying Technical Report (ISO/TR 15489-2, 2001) provide a framework and implementation guide for managing records and information in organisations today. Its appearance at the beginning of the 21st century confirms the importance attached globally to information and records.

1.3 Information as a corporate asset

Information has been referred to as the fourth resource after people, money and property (Best, 1996). More recently, the list of resources has grown to five and now includes technology (Fifth Resource Inc, 2004).

The information which an organisation produces and receives during the normal course of its business is recognised as a valuable and unique resource, which needs to be managed and exploited, as are other resources.

Each business operation generates information as a natural by-product. In some activities, for example an insurance claim, information is in fact the main product and, in the context of records management, the proof or evidence of the business processes. It costs money to produce the information and it should therefore be managed in the interests of efficiency. However, the information is unique to the business which produces it. On the one hand, it is an exclusive and valuable resource, but, on the other hand, it is potentially highly vulnerable because its loss may be irrecoverable and could result in the organisation going out of business.

Not all organisations have understood the importance of managing their information and their records appropriately. This lack of understanding has had varying consequences, as demonstrated by a number of high-profile cases in the press in the first years of the 21st century:

1. Enron affair (Boulton, 2002), where failure to manage their information and records appropriately contributed to the total collapse of the business with knock-on effects for its auditor (Arthur Andersen).
2. One of the world's largest media companies lost a legal case against an individual (ZyLAB, 2002). They were not able to corroborate their claim that the documents in question had been destroyed as part of their routine information management operations, thus calling into doubt the basis of their case.
3. The March 2002 Audit Commission briefing *Data remember - improving the quality of patient-based information in the NHS* (Audit Commission, 2002) revealed that there was room for improvement in almost all hospital trusts in England in their methods of recording information. In this context, lack of accurate information available to all of the clinicians involved with individual patients can adversely affect the consistency of care provided.

4. The landmark decision in Australia in the case McCabe vs. BAT (Slater & Gordon, 2002) exposed the illegal practice of using a records retention policy to destroy records that might implicate an organisation in the future.

There was however an initiative in the UK to improve the quality of managing information in public and private organisations. The Hawley Committee on *Information as an Asset* was established in 1995 under the auspices of the KPMG IMPACT programme and produced a ten-point checklist of guidelines for boards of directors on managing the information asset (Hawley Committee, 1995). The checklist firmly placed information on the board's agenda. It underlined the need for organisations to:

- create information
- use information
- manage and protect information against risk

as a unique business resource, in compliance with legal and other regulatory and ethical requirements. The list emphasizes not only the importance of the quality but also the quantity of the information produced, as well as recognising the relative and variable value of different information assets.

These guidelines remain valid as a macro level guide. The Department of Health (2003) has developed a similar checklist, which in addition covers the people aspects of information management.

Records, whether they are stored in electronic form, on paper or in other media, are the key manifestation of an organisation's unique information asset. Records are carriers of the information which a business needs in order to operate on a day-to-day basis. Many of the points on the checklists above relate directly to records management practices and thus confirm records management as a major element of information management within organisations.

An organisation's approach to records management needs therefore to be linked to and integrated with its core business activities. It also needs to embrace the world of rapid change and technological dominance which characterises the e-environment. However, as Bennett (1994) stated over a decade ago, but which is none the less valid today:

> "the issues which drive the organisation should also be those which drive effective records management. We need to link the RM process to issues that matter to management."

The size and extent of the information and records management challenge can be highlighted by some telling statistics. Each year about five exabytes of new information are created (an exabyte is 10 to the power 18) or the equivalent of 17 million books (Lyman, 2003).

From this study, some other important facts emerge:

- 92% of new information is stored on magnetic media.
- Each person in the world produces about 800 megabytes of recorded information per year.
- The volume of information printed on paper is increasing, with the majority in the form of office documents or postal mail. So much for the paperless office!
- Email produces more than 400,000 terabytes of new information each year. This equates to 31 billion emails a year.

Not all of this information constitutes records but much of it is the by-product of business activities and therefore has the potential to be a record. In addition, these statistics only relate to newly created information. However, whether created new or already in existence, not all records need to survive, or at least not beyond a limited time. It is estimated that less than 5% of records will require long term or permanent preservation.

In 1997 McKinley reported that

- 85% of documents filed are never retrieved
- 50% of documents or more are duplicated in file systems

- 60% of files moved to document retention facilities should have been destroyed instead
- 20% of a worker's time may be spent filing and retrieving important documents.

And more recently a survey by Lexmark Inc (www.creativematch. co.uk/viewNews/?90924) indicated that the average worker prints 10,000 sheets of paper each year at work and a document is printed 19 times during its life. Perhaps it is not surprising that 13% of accountants said it took them up to 10 minutes to find a document *on their desk.*

In order to decide which part of this information needs to survive, we first need to know which part of it represents records. However, before exploring what a record is and its purpose and value, this is a good time to distinguish between information management and records management and to consider knowledge management, another concept that involves managing information.

1.4 Information management vs. records management vs. knowledge management

The broadest term is sometimes considered to be information management. However, the term information management is defined in different ways by different people:

- librarians and information scientists are more likely to focus on the information which is being managed and the people using the information
- computer specialists will concentrate on the systems and the technology.

Whichever emphasis is put on it, the term information management encompasses the management of

- information of all types
- internally produced or externally acquired, and

- irrespective of the medium on which it is delivered and managed.

If this is the case then records management is part of information management. In particular, it is that part dealing with *internally* generated proprietary information i.e. the information that is an important and unique resource for the organisation producing it.

The debate about where records management fits within information management is important, not least because information is now accepted and recognised as a vital resource for organisations of all types. The key, however, is to ensure that the value of the asset of business records as information carriers is recognised. This will then determine the approach to records management, which needs to underline the critical role that managing records plays in contributing to the efficiency and success of the organisation.

If records management is part of information management, where does knowledge management fit? Like records management, knowledge management focuses on a unique resource i.e. the knowledge base of the organisation. This knowledge base resides, in part, in the heads of the employees, i.e. tacit knowledge. It also exists in the organisation's recorded information relating to the work of the organisation i.e. explicit knowledge. In the former it is a question of providing records of where the knowledge exists (i.e. who knows what). In the latter, it is the records of the organisation. This view of knowledge management clearly demonstrates that knowledge management depends on records management. They need to work hand in hand to meet business objectives. This idea is captured very succinctly by Best (BIP 0025:1, 2002):

"Records are repositories of the organisation's accumulated knowledge about itself, its suppliers and its customers. ...Over time records collections or series come to contain masses of information about trends through time, whether around processes, transactions or people.

They therefore provide management with predictive possibilities for extrapolation which were not previously possible or were previously too expensive."

This view of the relationship of records to information to knowledge shows that records and their management contribute directly to the way in which organisations operate. It is therefore necessary to:

- know what a record is, and
- have a clear understanding of the purpose and the value of records in order to ensure that
  - there is a valid reason for creating each record
  - they are captured into a recordkeeping system
  - they are readily available when needed for consultation
  - they are kept for as long as they are needed, and no longer.

1.5 Purpose, value and role of records – evidence and information

1.5.1 The purpose of records

There are three main reasons for keeping records:

- for information (i.e. to ensure that operations are carried out appropriately and to aid decision-making)
- for evidence (i.e. as proof that your organisation routinely follows consistent practices and for use if the organisation is faced with a lawsuit, and as a record of social and historical events)
- for compliance (i.e. as proof that regulations have been applied).

A fourth reason for keeping records is for societal or cultural use where organisations and individuals outside the creating organisation may use them for historical, sociological, scientific or other research. In order to determine which of these categories apply to particular records, it is essential to understand and establish the *value* of each group of records. This is achieved by a process called *appraisal*. It determines the life of the record based on its value and is dealt with in detail in Chapter 6.

1.5.2 The value of records

Records can have both a *primary* and a *secondary* value. Their primary value relates to the immediate reason for which they are created. This primary value can fall into one of three categories:

1. Administrative i.e. value in relation to the role they play in the everyday operations of the business; examples would be records to do with routine correspondence, staff time-keeping, requisitions
2. Fiscal i.e. value in relation to financial matters; examples would include income and expenditure records, which would have administrative value while being processed but would gain fiscal value within the context of audit procedures, for the calculation of VAT liability for instance
3. Legal i.e. value as proof of compliance with statutory requirements; examples would be deeds and contracts or a Health and Safety certificate.

These values are determined by the nature of the business transactions which they record. So, for example, requesting payment by issuing invoices has both an administrative and fiscal value. In UK law any request for payment needs to be kept for six years plus the current financial year. Once this time has passed, the need to have evidence of the transactions is satisfied and the invoices can be destroyed.

Once the primary value has been satisfied some records will not be destroyed since they will have acquired a secondary value. Secondary value relates to a potential future use and can be one of two kinds:

1. Evidential
2. Informational or historical.

So, periodically for either evidential or historical reasons, a small number of records whose primary value has expired may be kept and preserved, for example the invoice for a special purchase or the last invoice to be issued prior to decimalisation.

We return to the value of records in later chapters but at this stage the key point to make is that records play a crucial role within every organisation. Every business activity, whether it involves a product, a service or an administrative task, has an information dimension which generates records. The set of documents or records related to each business activity needs to be identified and managed to ensure that:

- at every stage, the relevant information is available to document the process
- the records are kept for as long as necessary to comply with any legal or regulatory or corporate memory requirements.

For example, in a mail order company, the business process and the document set relating to an order are identified in Figure 1.

The customer order and despatch notes, as administrative records, will be kept until the order has been satisfied and the invoice paid. The customer order and invoice have fiscal value as financial records, as stated above, and will be retained until the end of the financial year for audit purposes. They, however, also have legal value and will need to be kept to comply with statutory requirements.

From this example we can see the need to understand and identify the role of each record in relation to the business process which it documents, and its value, so as to ensure that it is managed appropriately. In Chapter 3 we explore more fully how to manage records in your organisation.

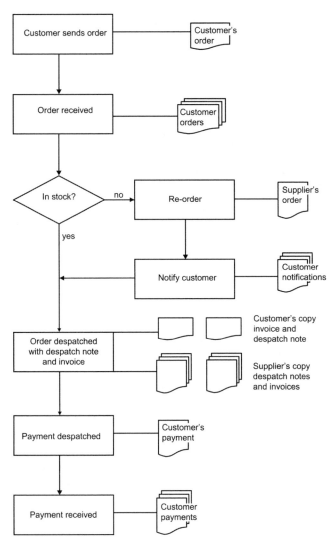

Figure 1 Mail order process

However, to conclude this chapter we need to establish the kinds of records we will be dealing with in the e-environment. So far we have not commented on records in specific media. As we said earlier, the vast majority of new information, and therefore by implication records, are nowadays electronic. But, as you look around your workplace and from the statistics quoted earlier, it is evident that records exist and continue to be created in a whole range of different media.

1.6 Record formats in the hybrid environment

In order to cover the kinds of records with which we are faced, we have divided them into three categories: electronic or digital records, paper records and records in other formats.

1.6.1 Electronic records, i.e. born digital and in different digital formats

First of all there are the records which are 'born digital'. By definition they are digital records because they are created by computers which process data as a numeric value, expressed in binary digits. There are the whole range of inputs to and outputs from all of the standard and specialist software systems which now proliferate in different organisations. They also come in a variety of different formats, such as web content, which might be multimedia and combine text, video and audio content.

Records in digital format will be a main focus of this guide as more and more this is the medium through which business in being conducted across the sectors. We use the term electronic records to describe these records created digitally.

1.6.2 Paper records

Many records still exist in paper form. In some cases this is a requirement. For example:

- the wet-ink signature on a mortgage deed confirms its authority and its authenticity
- to notify students of their results, a paper copy is sent via the mail.

The paper copy then constitutes the official record. Also, often in paper format, there are convenience copies, either printed out from a system or multiple photocopies of official records, which need to be identified and managed to reflect their purpose, i.e. working documents such as copies of minutes of meetings.

1.6.3 Records in other formats

Finally, there are those records which can be in a variety of different and very diverse formats, ranging from audio tapes and even human tissue, blood or geological samples. There are also the legacy systems, which are to be found in all organisations. These are the old systems which are perhaps no longer in day to day use but which still support the business operations. What these often have in common is that they are now managed electronically via database-type systems.

Records in the e-environment are therefore very diverse in nature but their management is central to the business activity, irrespective of the type of organisation. Electronic information is very easy to create, perhaps too easy to create. It is therefore essential that everyone working in the e-environment recognises and understands the challenges of managing records in this context and their own role in it. In the next chapter we consider what these challenges are.

First, to help you assess the drivers and information and records management context in your own organisation, consider the following questions and make notes about the current situation.

1.7 Issues to address – questions to answer

The organisational context

Question	Notes
What are the key business drivers in your organisation?	
How important are information and records to you organisation?	
How are information management, records management and knowledge management interrelated within your organisation?	
What kinds of legislation and regulation apply to your organisation? What are the implications for managing records	
Are all records considered to have the same value? If not, how is value determined?	
Which formats are used to store and manage records in your organisation	

Chapter 2

Challenges of the dynamic e-environment for records management

Before we can consider these challenges we need to establish some definitions.

2.1 Concepts and definitions

First what is a record? According to ISO 15489-1 (2001) records are

> "information created, received, and maintained as evidence and information by an organisation or person, in pursuance of legal obligations or in the transaction of business."

Specifically in the context of electronic records, The National Archives (The National Archives, 1999) offers the following definition:

> "A record is a specific piece of information produced or received in the initiation, conduct or completion of an institutional or individual activity. It comprises sufficient content, context and structure to provide evidence of that activity. It is not ephemeral: that is to say, it contains information that is worthy of preservation in the short, medium or long term."

From these definitions, we can see that records are carriers of information and proof of business activities. We can also identify the three aspects which are common and necessary to all records:

1. the *content* or message (i.e. the information they carry)
2. the *context* (i.e. the business purpose for which they were created and of which they provide evidence)
3. the *medium* and *structure* (i.e. their physical form and logical structure which identify and label their component parts and which give them a fixed form).

To be able to manage the records of your organisation it is essential to understand these three important characteristics, or aspects of 'recordness', that make up a record.

Records can range from:

- a letter to a contract
- an x-ray to an email message
- a geological sample to the Magna Carta

but all can be and need to be created and managed in relation to these three aspects.

The management of records is potentially a large task, even in relatively small organisations, for every organisation produces many thousands, if not millions, of records. This fact makes it impossible to manage records on an individual basis and indeed it is not necessary to manage them on an individual basis. Records relate to business activities and processes and can therefore be grouped together into what are usually described as *series*.

Shepherd and Yeo (2003) define a record series as follows:

"a series comprises the records of all of the activities that are instances of a single process. A series may be large or small: it is distinguished, not by size, but by the fact that it provides evidence of a particular process. If an activity takes place that is unique, rather than an instance of a process, its records form a series in their own right."

A record series groups together records which have been created to perform the same function or for the same purposes over a continuous period of time. The characteristics of the records in a records series can be summarised as:

- containing the same kind of information, although there may have been some changes over time
- having the same format, although there may have been evolution over time
- being organised in a sequence whether that be numerical, chronological or alphabetical
- remaining in existence for as long as the type of transaction to which they relate continues to be carried out within the organisation.

Take invoices as an example of a series:

- they contain the same information (supplier and customer details, items or services supplied and price etc) but over time the information content may evolve and include tax, such as VAT
- they will have the same standard format in terms of structure and physical form but over time may have moved from one paper size to another (credit card and utility invoices are good examples here) or may become issued and actioned electronically in the case of an e-commerce or e-business system
- they will either be physically arranged in a sequence, perhaps by invoice number or date issued, or retrievable in such a sequence, and finally
- they will exist as long as products or services are supplied and charged.

A series would only cease to exist as a result of the disappearance of the transaction type with which it was associated; similarly a new series would imply the establishment of a new function, activity or process and therefore new transactions within the organisation. Some categories of record series are common to all organisations because some functions and activities are common to all organisations, for example record series associated with human resources management, health and safety, office administration as well as financial management. This would include:

- recruitment
- audits and inspection of facilities
- time recording
- accounts payable.

In addition, organisations will have other series which are specific to their own business sector:

- patient files in hospitals
- laboratory notebooks in scientific organisations
- clinical trial data in pharmaceutical companies
- policies in an insurance company, and
- client files in a firm of chartered accountants.

And you can choose the level of grouping records into series that makes sense in your organisation. For example, you might not consider invoices to be a single series on their own but part of a larger series called accounts payable which includes invoices, purchase orders, etc. This idea can be further extended so that, taking the example of the staff recruitment process, all of the series to do with announcing the post and all those to do with the administration of the interviews could be handled as two large groups rather than as individual series. This process of aggregation of related series can support more effective and efficient management of records in the e-environment, for example, via a file plan.

We have seen above that one key characteristic of records is their ability to offer proof of business activities. In order to fulfil their role as evidence, records need to have further characteristics to confirm their recordness, as specified in ISO 15489-1 (2001). They need to be *authentic, reliable* and have *integrity.* Finally they need to be *useable.*

In the records context *authenticity* means that:

- records are what they claim to be
- they are created or sent by the person who claims to have created or sent them
- they are created or sent at the time claimed (ISO 15489-1, 2001).

So, for example to ensure the authenticity of the minutes of a Board meeting, it needs to be clearly identified that they are the minutes of the stated meeting, and that they were created by the Secretary to the Board, as the authorised minute taker, on the date stated.

The condition of authenticity then needs to be combined with *reliability.* ISO 15489 (2001) confirms that a reliable record is one

"whose contents can be trusted as a full and accurate representation of the transactions, activities or facts that they attest and can be depended upon in the course of subsequent transactions or activities."

The reliability comes from the authority of the records. Their authority comes from the fact that the minutes are a 'true and accurate record' (as the phrase goes). An added element of reliability results from the signature of the Chairperson at the following meeting, which confirms that the members present confirmed the accuracy of the minutes of the previous meeting.

Ensuring the characteristic of *integrity* means making sure that the records are complete and have not been changed. So, in the case of the minutes of a meeting, their integrity is established if they have not been changed since created and will remain unchanged i.e. they are inviolate.

The final characteristic to be met is that of ***usability*** which links back to the defining characteristic of records as evidence of business transactions. A useable record is:

> "one that can be located, retrieved, presented and interpreted. It should be capable of subsequent presentation as directly connected to the business activity or transaction that produce it". (ISO 15489-1, 2001)

This characteristic of usability reinforces the whole purpose of keeping records which is to have them available as long as they are needed to support the business activity to which they relate.

These characteristics of ***content, context, structure, authenticity, reliability, integrity*** and ***usability*** apply to any item which is or needs to be a record, irrespective of the physical medium in which it is created. In the case of paper records, the issues of context (which might come from the letterhead), authenticity and reliability (which might be confirmed by a wet ink signature linking back to printed detail in a letterhead), integrity or inviolability (which would be evident because they had not been altered in any way) and usability can be easily checked and verified visually. This is also the case for records in other physical formats, not least because they are directly intelligible and interpretable by human beings.

However, this is by no means the case for electronic or e-records. Let us now consider how they are different and what the issues are that we need to understand in managing them.

1.2 E-records, their special nature and understanding the issues

The first thing to say is that, in order for an item of electronic information to be an e-record, it needs to fulfil all of the conditions of a record. So let us take each of these conditions in turn and consider the issues they raise for electronic records.

The first aspect is *content*. An e-record has *content* i.e. the information it presents or contains; but immediately we have a difference because the message is not directly human readable. It is only readable if the appropriate hardware and software are available to turn the bits or binary digits, i.e. strings of 0s and 1s, into human readable form.

Secondly, in terms of their *medium* and *structure*, they are not single distinct physical and fixed items like paper records. The bits are stored on a physical medium which might be, for example, a floppy disk, a hard disk, a CD-ROM or USB memory stick. But there is no fixed relationship between the bits and the medium. The bits can be moved from one medium to another without potentially damaging the content. The medium and the message are separated, unlike with paper and records in other formats, such as microfilm or audio tapes. In these cases the medium and the message are coextensive. Electronic records do have a physical structure but again it is not immediately visible. They exist as strings of bits which are recorded on a magnetic surface, but may not occupy the same physically adjacent space. They can potentially be scattered across different areas of the medium on which they are stored. On the one hand you do not have to worry about the technical detail, but what you do need to realise is the fact that the physical structure of electronic records does not confer integrity as it does in the paper world. This means that you cannot immediately see whether anything is missing or has been changed. Therefore it is essential to identify the internal structural elements of the record i.e. their *logical* rather than their *physical* structure.

These requirements shift the focus from the records to the recordkeeping system. The system captures, at the logical level, details of the functions and activities covered and what transactions need to be recorded. Only once the logical level is defined is the link made with the physical level item, whether it be a database, a file or even a combination of different files in a compound document, such as an annual report. An annual report might have linked to it a spreadsheet and image files or a web page with all of the wide range of types of files it might contain.

Having looked at the physical medium and structure of electronic records, this has taken us into the third key characteristic of recordness, which is *context*. As for all records, the context relates to the business operation from which the record results. With electronic records this relationship needs to be captured explicitly. So, if we think about an electronic spreadsheet which records expenditure against budget allocation, information about the project and about the operational unit needs to be added to ensure that the administrative context is captured.

But there is another aspect of context for e-records and that is the context of the system which produced them. This covers hardware and software and is an essential part of the e-record, as it will ensure ongoing access and management over time i.e. make them a useable record.

So for electronic documents to achieve recordness they need to be supplemented by additional information to provide what O'Shea (1996) calls

"a simple, integrated and non-redundant definition of the records."

This additional information is called *metadata* or data about data. Metadata is not unique to electronic records, as some items such as series name, creator, retention period are common to other record formats. What is different is the time at which the metadata is added and/or captured. In the paper world this is often at the time of archiving. With electronic records it needs to be at the time of *creation* not only to ensure that the items created will be intelligible and accessible in the future but also that they have the necessary characteristics as records, i.e. content, medium and structure, context, reliability and authenticity. One point to note, however, is that the addition of metadata can be automated either for single records or record series. We come back to metadata again later in this chapter.

The tests of authenticity and reliability are also essential for electronic records, but again raise issues. The issues of authenticity and reliability can be addressed by adding the appropriate metadata, for example the authority of the creator in relation to the transaction. However, integrity, which requires that records remain complete and unchanged, and usability, which requires that the records can still be read for as long as they are required, are major challenges.

So does standard office hardware and software help with the issue of the integrity of records? All organisations now use technology to produce information. Their aim is to use the technology to work as efficiently and as effectively as possible. Hence, the software products which have been developed have focused on providing maximum flexibility to enter, edit, move, copy and delete information and have made these operations available to everyone with a PC on their desk. In terms of business effectiveness, the technology is very successful because of the return on investment from the possibility of re-using information. To create and maintain records it is necessary to fix information and supplement the information with metadata to achieve all of the characteristics of recordness. These operations are not integral to or fully automated within the standard functionality of these standard office software products. It is not to say that these requirements cannot be achieved. In order to fix the record copy of an e-file it is possible to save it as read-only, which will ensure that it cannot be freely changed without the necessary access rights. Similarly, the properties facility in the Microsoft Office suite of programmes, accessible from the File menu, can be used to capture automatically metadata about filename, creator, date created, date of last modification, as well as allowing the addition of other metadata elements.

In Figure 2a, within Microsoft Word, some Summary elements of metadata for the text of this guide have been picked up automatically from the system. There are also further types of metadata relating to Date Created and the software product used, as can be seen in Figure 2b, both under 'Type' and via the icon.

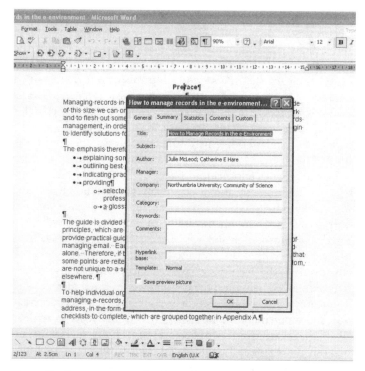

Figure 2a Summary properties for a Microsoft Word file

In addition there is some automatically generated statistical and content information. There is also a facility under Custom Properties to input additional elements such as date completed, destination, editor and disposition, which could cover destruction dates or transfer to archives instructions. These supplementary metadata elements have to be added manually. This requires not only additional resources and effort but a level of understanding about adding the data needed to create items which will satisfy requirements as records. In addition, the fact that they are added manually runs the risk that the additional elements may not always be added consistently, or indeed at all.

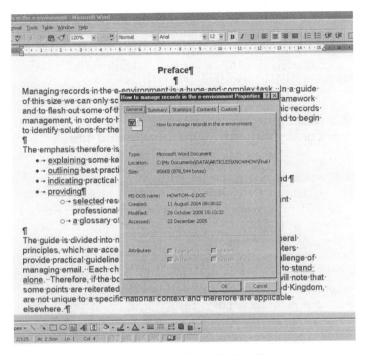

Figure 2b General properties for a Microsoft Word file

Despite these possibilities, the reality is that the majority of office software products do not offer recordkeeping functionality. They make it easy to add, change, delete and copy without leaving any trace of the modifications. There is also the issue of potential loss of some of this metadata when electronic information is migrated to new versions of software. For example the date data is very vulnerable, to the point that it is possible to result in a date created which is later than the date modified if the date/time has been reset on the PC.

In order then to be a true record, electronic records need to be created and captured with the relevant metadata. Let us now take the example of a signed letter on headed paper from the Head of Personnel offering a post to a successful applicant and compare it with the word-processed file from which it was produced in order to see how well the word-processed file meets the requirements of recordness.

2.3 Managing a paper letter vs. its corresponding word-processed file

Nowadays the majority of correspondence in organisations is created using word-processing software. A copy is then printed off and sent to the addressee for whom it becomes a record. The sender may make a photocopy and file it as their record or capture an e-file into an electronic records management system. What if no photocopy is made or e-copy filed, how good a record is the word-processed file?

The photocopy will have the same content as the paper record at the point at which it is copied but there is no guarantee that the content of the electronic version will not be subsequently changed, for example to use as the basis for the next job offer letter.

In terms of the medium and the structure, the photocopy will have a very clear structure and fixed layout as a letter with:

- the name, address, logo of the organisation and the name and position of sender printed on official headed paper
- the name and address of the addressee
- the date.

and of course the signature. By contrast the word-processed file may have the details of the person who word-processed the letter but that person may not necessarily be the sender nor will it have the signature. In addition, the date might have been set to pick up the date from the system. This means that the next time the file is opened the date will be updated to the new current date and not the date that the letter was created.

For the photocopy the context is confirmed, partly by the letter content and partly by the details of the sender. For the electronic version, the content is present but not fixed and the details of the sender may not be explicit. There might however be some clues from the automatic properties data.

So how does the electronic version meet the fundamental characteristics of recordness? It could perhaps be said to meet the test of reliability as it does relate to a job offer, but it would be very easy to change "successful" to "unsuccessful" without any obvious trace of the change being left. It is also vulnerable in terms of authenticity as it does not have the signature to match the name and job position on the headed paper. Its integrity is also in question because it is not fixed and bound inviolably to a physical medium.

This paints a bleak picture of the inadequacy of the word-processed file as an electronic record. However it is possible to make the word-processed file a valid record by capturing it into a system which keeps it as a record, i.e. has recordkeeping functionality. And this is where we come back to metadata and the key role of the recordkeeping system in the creation, capture and management of electronic records. In Chapter 3 we focus on how to manage records and in Chapter 7 we explore the different organisational and software solutions. Now, however, let us return to the challenge of the identification of relevant metadata.

Table 1 Comparative recordness of a photocopy of a letter and the wordprocessed file of a letter

	Photocopy	Wordprocessed file
Content	✔	?
Context	✔	✗
Structure	✔	✗
Authenticity	✔	?
Reliability	✔	✗
Integrity	✔	✗
Usability	✔	?

2.4 Role of metadata and functional requirements

Metadata is crucial for electronic records because it makes them complete as records. For metadata to guarantee complete electronic records, it needs to be captured at the point of creation of the record and added to later, for example if they are migrated to a new system. The quality of the metadata will determine the quality of the record, in terms of it being fit for purpose to:

- support business operations
- meet legal and other regulatory requirements.

The example of the word-processed letter demonstrates the range of metadata required for a very simple document that is the output of a single transaction. And the metadata needs not only to fix the record but also to allow it to be managed and remain available for as long as required, depending on its value.

In this chapter we are focusing on the challenges of the e-environment. But it is important to note that, across the world, a lot of very useful and helpful work has been done to explain the role of metadata in managing electronic records and to develop standard sets of metadata. In the wider context of developing systems for the e-environment there are sets of *functional requirements* so called because they provide detailed specifications for fully functioning recordkeeping systems which include metadata requirements.

Although much of the work has been done in the government sector and with a focus on the specification, selection and/or evaluation of electronic records management systems, it does provide generic guidelines which can apply in all organisations.

There are two notable examples of functional requirements which provide valuable guidance. First there is the MoReq (Model Requirements for the Management of Electronic Records) specification which relates to all organisations throughout Europe (2001). As its name suggests it is a model, generic specification which "focuses mainly on the functional management of electronic records by an Electronic Records Management System." (ERMS)

It identifies the core requirements for an ERMS, from the creation of the records to their final fate. It comprises a major section on the metadata needed to ensure that the records are created appropriately and maintained for as long as necessary.

In the UK The National Archives (2002) published their Functional Requirements for Electronic Records Management Systems 2002. It comprises three elements:

1. the functional requirements setting out the functionality required of a system
2. the metadata standard for compliant systems
3. a reference document covering the basic concepts.

Basically it provided a checklist of requirements for managing electronic records against which software products for electronic records management were tested and approved (www.nationalarchives.gov.uk/electronicrecords/reqs2002/approved.htm). However, in 2005 The National Archives announced it was to cease its testing programme and would not update its functional requirements document, instead supporting the ongoing development of MoReq.

Functional requirements and metadata are challenging issues in managing records in the e-environment. The relationship between records and the business processes to which they relate is key. There are issues of principle to establish at the strategic level, but also we need practical guidelines on how to make them work. The remainder of this guide combines strategic frameworks and models with guidelines and advice on practical systems and procedures.

Before moving on, it is time for you to reflect on these and the other challenges of managing electronic records in your organisation by considering and responding to the questions below.

2.5 Issues to address – questions to answer

Challenges of the dynamic electronic environment for records management

Question	Notes
What types of electronic records do you have in your organisation?	
How are they managed?	
Which metadata is captured automatically?	
Which metadata is added by the endusers?	
How was your system specified?	
Who specified your system?	
Did you use any of the sets of functional requirements mentioned in the text? If so, which one and why?	

Chapter 3

How to manage records in your organisation

3.1 Making the vision a reality

Given the value, importance and/or requirement to manage records for evidential, compliance and informational purposes, how can you manage records in your organisation in practice?

There are, in fact, a number of different approaches you can take based on the use of different models and frameworks and the way in which you implement them. We explore the main ones and the contexts in which each might be most appropriate, so that you can make the best choice for your organisation.

To transform the vision for managing your organisation's records into a reality it is important to recognise:

a. the drivers and the priorities
b. the systems and
c. the different views of those involved.

a. Drivers and priorities

The drivers and priorities, as we saw in Chapter 1, are important because they represent the strategic level of the organisation. They may be:

- legal or regulatory requirements
- a forthcoming audit by an external body

- a recent difficulty (for instance an embarrassing 'leak' of information or failure to find records for evidence in a legal or audit case)
- a merger or acquisition or a major new project.

The priorities will be, respectively:

- the records of those functions and activities covered by the law and regulations
- the audit
- the problem
- the merger/acquisition or the project.

Alternatively, the driver may be a relocation to new premises or the aftermath of a major disaster, in which case *all* records will need to be considered. In the case of a relocation particular priorities may be placed on saving space/money and therefore the destruction of records, especially paper records, which are no longer required and/or the design and introduction of new recordkeeping systems. In the case of a disaster then the identification of records vital for future business continuity and their protection and backup will be the priorities.

All of these drivers represent 'extremes', i.e. crisis or particular situations. Whilst they provide excellent not-to-be-missed opportunities for driving forward records management in an organisation, they should not be seen as the only ones for making the vision a reality. Smart organisations will recognize that "good recordkeeping is fundamental to good business" (State Records New South Wales, 2003). In other words it should be the *norm* for organisations to manage their records well as a routine part of their daily business operations. Whilst records management may not in itself be a strategic function for most organisations, it can and should support those functions that are strategic.

b. Systems

At the practical and operational level, systems play a very important role in implementing the vision. It is particularly important in the electronic environment to recognise the nature and variety of these systems. Some may be formalised and they may be totally electronic, paper based or hybrid. They may or may not be true recordkeeping systems but rather data, information or document management systems. They will have a records management role or dimension, or the potential for one, and therefore will need the functionality to support the creation, use and management of records with the necessary characteristics explained in Chapter 2.

Some systems will be simply 'custom and practice', for example signed approval of annual leave which is then recorded on wall charts or in group diaries. They may be examples of best practice but not be formally documented. In such cases written policies and/or procedures are needed to ensure that they are adequate. And of course systems to be managed will fall into one of three main categories:

a. legacy systems
b. current systems, and
c. systems which are yet to be designed or selected and implemented.

The latter offer a particularly important opportunity for influencing the future approach to managing records in the electronic environment.

c. People – the views of those involved

What bridges the gap between strategy and operations? What binds these two levels together? What can make or break the successful implementation of any system? The answer to all of these questions is *people*.

If you are the records manager, or the person who has been given overall responsibility for managing records in your organisation, then your view of the requirements will be different to most other people's in the organisation. Your view necessarily must be holistic whereas the views of other individuals will tend to be local or parochial, i.e. relate to the things that matter directly to them. They will be most interested in the records they create and need to access and hence the systems for managing these. But they need to recognise that there is a bigger picture, the one you and your senior management supporters see. They too must see that they, and the records and systems they create and use, are an integral part of this bigger picture.

Having established that these three issues – drivers, systems and people – are crucial aspects of moving from principles to practice, we need to look at the ways to approach managing records in *your* organisation. The terms models, frameworks, paradigms, methodologies and strategies are all used in the field. Some are essentially interchangeable whilst others are embedded in a particular concept or idea. For the purposes of this guide the terms ***models, frameworks*** and ***methodologies*** will be used and their particular meanings within this context will be explained. Your chosen combination of models, frameworks and methodology, from the alternatives available, will form the approach you take to managing records for your organisation.

3.2 Models for managing records

What do we mean by a model within the context of records management? A model is based on a concept which can be represented in some diagrammatic form. There are two main models for managing an organisation's records - the lifecycle model and the continuum model - each having different origins and a different focus. Much has been written about both models at the level of principle as well as practice, but it is not appropriate in this guide to add to that literature. Instead the aim here is to distil the essence of each one and to highlight their particular strengths for the management of your organisation's records in the e-environment.

3.2.1 The lifecycle model

This model, developed at the National Archives of the United States of America in the 1930s, is based on the concept that a record has a life. It is born (i.e. is created), it lives (i.e. is used and maintained) and it 'dies' (i.e. is disposed of).

Described in this way the lifecycle model suggests that records move from one phase to another, over time, in a linear rather than a cyclical way, i.e. from creation to active use then semi/inactive use and ultimately disposition. If the model is to be a cycle, then disposition cannot simply be synonymous with destruction at the 'end' of the life. So, records may be re-born, as in new versions, or they may be permanently preserved and used to support the creation of entirely different and new records. Disposition can result in either destruction, transfer or indefinite (permanent) retention. Figure 3 illustrates this model as applied to the word-processed letter discussed in Chapter 2.

Records that are no longer required by the organisation should be destroyed. Records that still need to be retained for a finite period but are no longer needed on a day-to-day basis (e.g. financial records which must be kept for six years beyond

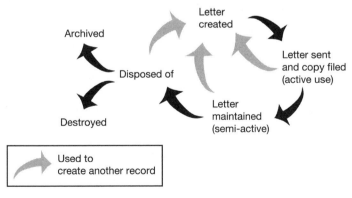

Figure 3 The lifecycle of a word-processed letter

the financial year in which they were created) may be transferred to inactive storage, if they are in paper format, or stored 'offline' on some optical or digital medium if they are in electronic format. Those records that are of historical value may be stored in a particular e-location or physically transferred to archives for permanent retention. The latter lead to the traditional role of archives as a repository for the preservation of inactive records disposed of by their originators but, in the e-environment, physical transfer to archives may or may not be required. What will be required is the designation of an e-location(s) for permanent retention.

The lifecycle model was developed in the world of paper records, although its continued use means that it has been applied within the electronic environment. Its focus is on the records themselves and the different roles and responsibilities for managing them as they live out their lives in the different phases, triggered by time and their location. Its strength is that it is simple to grasp and it lends itself to powerful imagery and comparison as in, for instance, the birth, death and re-birth of plants, people and other organisms. But its simplicity is potentially also its weakness.

Not only are records created, they are also designed (i.e. conceived) and need to be captured into a recordkeeping system if they are to be used and maintained. So, the lifecycle should begin with a phase akin to birth control and family planning to avoid the creation of unwanted records and accumulation of 'documents'. There needs to be a conscious decision-taking process each time a new record is created because, once it has been created, it will have a life which needs to be managed. Conscious decision-making about which business transactions need to be documented will ensure that all *necessary* records are created and/or captured where previously they have not been as, for example, with an unrecorded telephone call or a verbal decision made between colleagues. The creation phase of the lifecycle is very important because it is here that the management of the record needs to be established (based on the business function, activity or process of which it is a part). Taking the right decisions at the point of creation in terms of:

- appraisal and retention
- storage location and medium
- metadata and classification

will facilitate access to, use of, longevity, preservation as well as timely destruction or disposition of the record. In the e-environment it is particularly crucial to address the creation phase if:

a. the power of technology and the opportunities it offers are to be harnessed in the design of data, information, document and recordkeeping systems, and
b. the creation, capture, use, long term access and destruction of electronic records is to be managed.

Records captured on electronic media will not wait patiently for attention.

In 1995 Rothenberg first suggested that:

"it is only slightly facetious to say that digital information lasts forever – or five years, whichever comes first." (Rothenberg, 1995)

And in 2002 he felt the prediction was still "the best we can say" (Rothenberg, 2002). This relatively short life expectancy, due to media decay and media instability, systems and/or software obsolescence, has already been borne out in practice. By 2002 the multimedia version of the Domesday Book created in 1986 was almost lost because the special BBC microcomputers, which were used to read the 12-inch laser discs on which the information about life in Britain at that time had been recorded, were obsolete (McKie and Thorpe, 2002). Meanwhile the original Domesday Book compiled in 1086 resides in good condition at The National Archives,

Kew. (Fortunately the CAMiLEON project has rescued the information, but, of course, preserving it into the future will still be a challenge. (CAMiLEON, 2003)). We return to this incident together with other examples in Chapter 5 within the context of risk management

If this model is to be used in the electronic environment it is absolutely vital to take account of the interrelationships that exist between the different phases in the records lifecycle. No phase of the life cycle can be treated in isolation, all phases need to be managed in a co-ordinated way and the management processes need to begin before the records are created, ideally at the point of systems design and development, so that when records are created there is a system into which they can be captured. This means that the roles and responsibilities of the various people involved in the different phases – from systems designers and administrators to records creators to records managers and archivists – need to be clearly understood and accepted. And these people need to work together in partnership to be successful.

So, the model is not necessarily redundant in the electronic environment; it has its supporters (Bantin, 1998), but may need to be adapted or applied differently.

3.2.2 The records continuum model

Three key names are usually associated with the records continuum model – Jay Atherton, Ian McLean and Frank Upward. Without examining the detailed history of its development, it was Atherton (1985-86) who first explicitly referred to a records continuum *model* although it is to McLean that the earliest use of the word 'continuum' has been attributed (Piggott and McKemmish, 1994). But it is Upward's analysis of continuum thinking at the end of the 20th century and his diagrammatic representation of the model which has the greatest potential for influencing its use as an approach to managing records in the electronic environment (Upward, 2000). (For more detail about the model's development Flynn (2001) provides a very good overview).

First presented in 1996 (Upward, 1996) the records continuum model is a model for the complex, dynamic electronic environment, going beyond McLean and Atherton's concerns about the artificial division of activities and responsibilities between records management and archives. Upward (2000) asks the key question:

"What will recordkeeping and archiving processes be like when the location of the material matters less than its accessibility, when records no longer have to move across clear boundaries in space or time to be seen as part of an archive, and when an understanding that records exist in space-time, not space and time, is more intuitively grasped by any practitioner?"

Upward's model addresses the fact that, in the electronic environment, records are 'virtual', logical entities or objects rather than physical ones, that recordkeeping is (or needs to be) integral to business functions and processes and that records are being created and used in technology-based systems.

In diagrammatic form the model is represented by four 'continua' (originally represented by axes) and four concentric circles (Upward, 2000). The four continua – transactional, identity, evidential and recordkeeping – represent major records management themes. The circles represent the 'dimensions' of the continuum – create, capture, organise and pluralise – and relate to processes.

A much simplified version of the model, focusing on the dimensions only, is represented in the following diagram. Using the word-processed letter of a job offer as an example, the **create** dimension involves entering the text; *capture* involves adding metadata to confer its recordness and saving the letter; *organise* involves placing the e-file in the recordkeeping system as a part of a relevant series or group; and **share and**

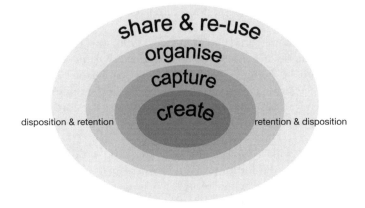

Figure 4 Simplified version of the continuum model focusing on the processes for managing records

re-use (or pluralise) means the letter is available to consult and could be used as the basis for a new letter or other new record.

Rather than focusing on the records and their 'status' and different points in time, this model focuses on ***processes*** and ***activities***, which fits well with the electronic environment where ***systems*** become the centre point. Whilst the continuum model has been used in academic teaching and research contexts, there is little published evidence to date that the model has made a significant impact in practice, but this could change. And the model can certainly be used to check that processes have been completely documented (Reed, 2005).

3.3 Roles, responsibilities and repositories

Continuum thinking has, however, served to highlight an important difference in the nature or approach to managing records in the electronic environment. Because records are *logical* rather than physical, as in the paper environment, their location can be *'virtual'*. Records will not necessarily need to be amassed in a single or limited number of locations (such as physical records centres and archives), but could live out their lives in virtual, distributed electronic collections, records centres and archives. This is referred to as the 'post-custodial' or 'distributed custody' model as distinct from the 'custody model' of the past where records managers and archivists were the custodians of the records.

The distributed custody model highlights the shared nature of the roles and responsibilities for recordkeeping in the electronic environment. Record creators are responsible for creating and "keeping accurate and complete records of their activities" (ISO 15489-1, 2001) and the responsibility for preservation and access over time may be devolved to them or at least nominated roles. In this environment the role of records managers and archivists covers:

- the development of policy, strategy and procedures
- the specification and/or design, implementation and maintenance of recordkeeping systems
- training
- monitoring and evaluation.

Increasingly, records managers and archivists are becoming what Bearman and Hedstrom (1993) referred to as the 'steerers' rather than the 'rowers' i.e. the facilitators and directors rather than do-ers.

In addition, two other groups of people have particular responsibilities for managing records. First, systems administrators are responsible for "ensuring that all documentation is accurate, available and legible" (ISO 15489-1, 2001) and, second, senior management and business executives are responsible for "supporting the application or records management policies throughout the organisation" (ISO 15489-1, 2001).

3.4 ISO 15489 – a framework for records management

ISO 15489 represents the consensus on international best practice in records management. It comprises two parts:

- ISO 15489-1:2001 Information and documentation – records management. Part 1: General, and
- ISO/TR 15489-2:2001. Information and documentation – records management. Part 2: Guidelines.

In simple terms Part 1 (the standard itself) is the 'what' and Part 2 (the technical report) the 'how'.

The standard highlights the benefits of good records management, which will be helpful for anyone needing to sell the concept to management. It stresses the role and importance of policy in managing records (covered later in this chapter) and confirms that *everyone* in an organisation has some responsibility for managing records, but that some groups of people have particular or special roles, as just discussed.

ISO 15489 provides guidance on the requirements for both *records* and *records systems* (the term records systems rather than recordkeeping systems is the preferred term in the standard). As discussed in Chapter 2 records must be authentic, reliable, have integrity and be usable. To achieve this the standard advocates the implementation of a *comprehensive records management programme* that includes everything from the determination of which records need to be created for each business process through to identifying and assessing opportunities where better records management could improve business efficiency, effectiveness and quality (ISO 15489-1, 2001).

Records systems must be reliable, compliant, comprehensive, systematic and also have integrity. The standard incorporates the DIRKS or DIRS methodology for the design and implementation of records systems (National Archives of Australia, 2001) and addresses issues such as:

- documenting records transactions
- physical storage medium and protection
- distributed management
- conversion and migration
- access, retrieval and use
- retention and disposition.

A major section of the standard covers what are described as records management processes and controls. These include:

- capturing and registering records into a records system
- retention management
- classifying and indexing records
- records storage and handling
- access
- tracking, and last but certainly not least,
- documenting records management processes

In addition monitoring and auditing as well as training are covered, albeit very briefly. What is not covered is the management of archival records within archival institutions.

In its current form the standard is not a compliance standard; however, it provides a rigorous framework, or underlying structure, for managing records in any format and any sector, public or private, to meet both organisational and regulatory requirements.

Although ISO 15489 is intended to be used by any individual in any organisation with a duty to create and maintain records as well as by records management professionals, it is probably the latter group who will gain most from the standard as it is presented. However, to help the other groups of personnel some of the national member bodies of ISO who have adopted the standard have already developed further publications. In the United Kingdom, for example, BSI (the British Standards Institute) has published three practical guides BIP 0025, Parts 1, 2 and 3 (2002-2003). The first is aimed at senior management and focuses on making the case for implementing a records management programme using ISO 15489. It includes some very useful scenarios which highlight the benefits of good records management and the potential risks as a result of not managing records. The second focuses on the design and implementation of a records system by synthesising the essential elements of the DIRKS methodology and making it more readily useable by a range of organisations. It includes flowcharts and checklists to use in the process. And the third considers performance management as a means of ensuring the sustainability of a records management programme.

The ISO standard can provide the underlying structure, the framework or the skeleton (the 'what') onto which the flesh or the details, the processes and the systems for managing your organisation's records (the 'how') can be built. What is then needed to implement this is a more comprehensive set of procedures or system of methods i.e. a methodology, which leads us on to DIRKS.

3.5 DIRKS – a methodology for designing and implementing recordkeeping systems

The DIRKS methodology first appeared in the Australian records management standard (AS 4390, 1996) and was jointly developed by the National Archives of Australia and the State Records Authority of New South Wales. The methodology is fully documented in the DIRKS Manual of which there are currently two versions. One is from the National Archives of Australia (2001) and the other from State Records New South Wales (2003). Both manuals share the same theoretical basis and approach to recordkeeping but the former is Commonwealth specific and the latter reflects the specific jurisdictional needs of the public sector in New South Wales. The methodology and the manuals are, however, broadly applicable to any organisation in any sector, including the private sector.

As its full name (Design and Implementation of Record-Keeping Systems) suggests DIRKS has a particular focus and, not surprisingly perhaps, has much in common with generic systems analysis and design methodology and project management. Because of this, one of its strengths is that it will make sense to non-records professionals, in particular IT personnel and project managers. But, in addition, it has been specifically developed for the records management context and "is a means of building good recordkeeping into your organisation" (State Records New South Wales, 2003).

The DIRKS methodology helps to:

> "transform business information systems that should be managing evidence of their operations into recordkeeping systems." (State Records New South Wales, 2003)

This means ensuring that systems produce and maintain complete, accurate and reliable evidence of business transactions by building the necessary recordkeeping characteristics of reliability, integrity, compliance, comprehensiveness, fixity and accessibility (State Records New South Wales, 2003). The methodology comprises the following eight steps:

Step A: Preliminary investigation
Step B: Analysis of business activity
Step C: Identification of recordkeeping requirements
Step D: Assessment of existing systems
Step E: Identification of strategies for recordkeeping
Step F: Design of a recordkeeping system
Step G: Implementation of a recordkeeping system
Step H   Post-implementation review

Steps A-C are about 'doing the right things' whilst Steps D-H are about 'doing things right' (National Archives of Australia, 2001). Together they provide a rigorous approach to the design and implementation of recordkeeping systems. The manual is comprehensive and its size might suggest to some that it can only be used by large organisations with significant resources, but, as the State Records version of the manual points out:

> "In its implementation, DIRKS can be whatever you want it to be. You can use the guidance in this manual to support a multi-million dollar exercise or a quiet afternoon's reflection" (State Records New South Wales, 2003).

The methodology and the manual can be used to:

- build better recordkeeping
- develop recordkeeping tools
- obtain general support and guidance
- achieve compliance
- build skills and knowledge.

State Records New South Wales' DIRKS Manual (2003) expands on some of these: for example building better recordkeeping might include:

- ensuring the creation and capture of records
- managing your vital records appropriately
- managing records access and security
- improving business processes and systems
- developing new systems with adequate recordkeeping functionality
- facilitating the purchase and implementation of off-the-shelf records management software
- ensuring records are kept of outsourced functions.

Developing recordkeeping tools might include:

- creating and implementing a keyword thesaurus
- creating and implementing a retention and disposal authority
- specifying and applying recordkeeping metadata.

And support and guidance covers such things as:

- developing a disposal authority
- developing a records management policy
- commenting on recordkeeping requirements of a new in-house-designed business system
- developing a training programme for email management, and
- contributing to the implementation of the ISO 9000 (2000) quality management standard.

Immediately, this demonstrates the flexibility and broad applicability of the DIRKS methodology. But another important aspect of its flexibility is that you do not necessarily have to conduct the eight steps in the process sequentially. Parts of some steps could be conducted at the same time as others and the starting point will depend on the current status of records management within your organisation. Both manuals provide suggestions as to how DIRKS might be used (National Archives of Australia, 2001; State Records New South Wales, 2003).

3.6 Choosing the best approach for your organisation

Having explored the two key records management models, a best practice framework and a recordkeeping systems design methodology, what is the best way for you to manage records in your organisation?

To decide, you need to consider the following questions:

- Is the focus to be on the records and their lifecycle management, i.e. what your organisation has and how it should be managed, by whom and through time?
- Is the focus to be on what the organisation does (i.e. its functions), how it does it (i.e. its activities and processes) and how the evidence of that is managed (i.e. its records)?

- Should the elements of a records management pro-gramme, as identified in ISO 15489, be the guiding principle?
- Can any of the processes and controls of ISO 15489, such as the business classification system, be used?
- Who will have which role and responsibilities for mana-ging records?
- Could the eight systems analysis and design principles of DIRKS be used to form the basis of an approach?

All of these questions relate to the use of the whole or parts of the models, framework and methodology. But, in addition to choosing from these options, there is another very impor-tant and practical decision to be made about your overall approach which will be influenced by, for example, your organisation's priorities, available resources, style and culture. Two quite different overall approaches to managing your organisation's records are the ***records management programme*** approach and the ***project-based*** approach.

The records management programme approach could be described as a ***holistic*** approach. Backed up by a records management policy, such a programme is a 'prescription' for records management and therefore must have a structure from which to grow. The ISO standard provides a framework and a blueprint for such a structure (ISO 15489-1, 2001) which can be developed to suit your particular situation.

At the opposite end of the spectrum is the project-based approach. This could be described as the ***targeted*** approach which might focus on specific aspects of records management of particular concern in your organisation. It might be used to achieve some 'quick wins' and demonstrate the benefits of records management, e.g. records of a particular business process or a legacy collection. But it too should be founded on policy. Initially these may be existing policies in your organisation which are not explicitly about records manage-ment but which have a records management dimension, for example your information policy, business continuity or risk management policy, email policy or health and safety policy. Alternatively, the foundations of a project-based approach might be the organisation's two-to-five year plan, its vision or particular targets.

Determining which approach is best for your organisation is an important first step. It establishes your strategy or game plan. Generally speaking, unless your organisation has suffered a disaster, has especially enlightened senior management or is very heavily regulated, then records management will not be a top priority. Your challenge is to bring it onto senior management's radar screen and make it attractive, beneficial and easy to incorporate into daily business operations, in other words be 'the norm'. To do so, it makes sense to swim with the tide rather than against it, i.e. to adopt the approach which makes most sense for your particular organisation.

3.7 Monitoring, measuring and managing performance

How can you measure change, progress, successes and/or compliance? How do you know if what you set out to achieve has been achieved and how well it has been done? How can you demonstrate the benefits to the organisation? Monitoring and auditing, followed by modification where necessary, is an important aspect of implementing records management and ensuring its sustainability.

ISO/TR 15489-2 (2001) provides some guidance on what and how to monitor records systems and/or programmes, but far more is available in BIP 0025:3 (2003), one of the BSI publications mentioned earlier. This begins by highlighting the important distinction between 'measurement' and 'management' – the former being concerned with evaluating efficiency and effectiveness against a set of agreed outcomes, the latter being concerned with *using* the information to understand what is happening and make changes where necessary. Both are essential.

BIP 0025:3 (2003) advocates measuring a records management programme, or records system, in terms of:

- efficiency – doing things right
- effectiveness – doing the right things, and
- impact – changes or outcomes.

Two other measures are *economy*, i.e. resource utilization, and *ease-of-use* which in part may fall within these three but can be explicitly identified.

Efficiency compares inputs with outputs, usually in terms of time or money. So the cost of online storage and preservation systems, speed of retrieval or time spent on destruction might be measured. In each case the unit cost might be very favourable in comparison with some benchmark and hence be seen to be efficient. But what if many of the records are being stored for longer than is required, what if copies on back-up tapes haven't been destroyed or records have been migrated to new systems when there is no real need to do so? In each case the records are not being managed effectively. Measuring the effectiveness of a programme or system is concerned with assessing whether or not it is delivering what is needed. When this involves the implementation of a new process or system, for instance an electronic document and records management system (EDRMS), this might also incorporate the ease-of-use measure.

And finally, what is the impact on the organisation? What have been the changes, outcomes or consequences as a result of a records management initiative, be they positive, negative, anticipated or unanticipated? Impact measures must relate to the organisation's overall strategic direction and be capable of demonstrating the benefits of good records management. Some impact measures may be difficult to quantify, but others can be expressed in economic terms. Examples might include:

- legislative/regulatory compliance - for instance the ability to meet freedom of information requests without the need for additional human resource

- space – fewer copies of records stored, eliminating the need to purchase more (online) server space and/or enabling a relocation to smaller premises
- human resource utilisation/job satisfaction - less time spent on processing and filing, less time wasted looking for records and more time spent on the core role.

Whether you adopt the 'four-Es' or 'two-Es-and-one-I' approach to performance measurement and management, the cost of doing it must not be forgotten. Therefore a *realistic* set of measures needs to be selected and changed as required. It may be important to measure the impact of a particular initiative in the short term but not the longer term. Measures are not fixed forever. And a crucial part of performance management is not only using the measures with those directly involved, but also communicating the developments, successes and progress with a wider audience in the organisation and possibly outside.

One trap to avoid is to *justify* a records management programme or system solely on savings. Although savings may be made in some areas, investment in time and money will be required.

"Good records management practice is an investment for the organisation, although it could easily be viewed as an overhead. The need to demonstrate the tangible returns of this investment is crucial. ... Ultimately there are likely to be financial savings but there is first a need to invest to save." (BIP 0025:3, 2003)

As Penn, Pennix and Coulson (1994) put it a decade ago, records management is an 'invested overhead'. Records should be managed because of their information value, as a unique resource for organisations, and potentially for wider society, and as a source of evidence to support and defend its operations. Any overall savings may be viewed as a bonus.

3.8 Success factors

The success of managing records in your organisation depends on a combination of factors:

- choosing the right approach for your organisation based on knowing your organisation, i.e. understanding the drivers and priorities, the people, processes, systems and stakeholders
- integrating records management with business functions, activities and processes
- getting buy-in, commitment and co-operation, from all staff but especially from senior management at the start
- recognising the roles and responsibilities of every member of staff
- managing change by involving people, listening and providing support, training and resources - people need to understand why they are being asked to perform a certain activity or do things differently rather than just told to do it
- communicating at all stages of the planning and implementation cycle, and
- evaluating the programme effectively in conjunction with internal audit to set standards and define specifications.

A records management programme provides an implementation tool, but it needs to be managed at a strategic level and it will only be successful if it is aligned with the aims and objectives of the organisation to which it refers.

3.9 Issues to address – questions to answer

How to manage records in your organisation

Question	Notes
Who currently has responsibilities for managing records in your organisation? Which other individuals/groups need to be identified as having responsibilities?	
What is the best way for your organisation to approach managing its records? Using: <ul><li>the records (lifecycle) model</li><li>the process (continuum) model</li><li>ISO 15489</li><li>DIRKS</li><li>a records management programme</li><li>a project approach</li></ul>	
How important is performance management for records management in your organisation?	
What will be the key success factors for managing your organisation's records?	

Chapter 4

Managing Records for Legal and Regulatory Compliance

High profile cases serve to highlight the potentially serious consequences, for organisations and individuals alike, of inadequate or inappropriate management of records. Recent examples include the alleged financial mismanagement and shredding of documents in the American oil company Enron, referred to in Chapter 1, which resulted in the demise of a leading management and accountancy company Arthur Andersen, the similar scandal at WorldCom where senior executives lost their jobs, and the call for the resignation of a chief constable following the discovery that personal data about one of the accused in the Soham murder investigation had not been retained and was not available to be shared.

Two of these events prompted the United States Congress to pass new legislation, the Sarbanes-Oxley Act 2002, or SOX, empowering the Securities and Exchange Commission (SEC) to impose strict rules regarding corporate governance for companies listed in the USA. Many of the rules relate to the provision of documentation regarding financial procedures and reporting. The third prompted the UK Information Commissioner to review the guidance provided on the interpretation of retention and use of personal data under the Data Protection Act (1998).

Managing records for legal and regulatory compliance is an important part of any records management programme, but where to begin?

4.1 Legal requirements

"All organisations need to identify the regulatory environment which affects their activities and requirements to document their activities." (ISO 15489-1, 2001)

This is an easy statement to make, but the range and number of laws and regulations which have implications for record-keeping is so great that it is challenging to achieve. In a small guide such as this it is impossible to cover all the relevant legal requirements and it would be inappropriate to attempt to do so, given the fact that they vary according to the business sector and constantly change. The aim therefore is to identify only key types and highlight some particularly relevant pieces of legislation that affect many organisations as examples of the kind of requirements and implications for managing records.

But, to begin, what are the key issues of legal and regulatory compliance and implications for your organisation? Assuming that your organisation is aware of its legal and regulatory obligations, then it must be able to "provide adequate evidence of its compliance with the regulatory environment in the records of its activities" (ISO 15489-1, 2001). And this will require policies and procedures to be in place for:

- the creation of records to capture the evidence
- storage, access and use, including right to and limitations on access to records and/or their content, and indexing to facilitate retrieval
- retention and preservation, including transfer to other organisations, and
- appropriate and timely disposal when no longer required to be retained.

Whilst some laws and regulations contain *explicit* record-keeping requirements, for instance the need to create specific types of records and the need to keep records for a specific length of time, many more contain *implicit* requirements for recordkeeping.

4.1.1 Retention

Every jurisdiction has laws and regulations which have record-keeping implications and compliance may be a legal requirement, i.e. mandatory, or best practice. Explicit retention require-ments include company accounting records (three years for private companies and six years for public companies, subject to company insolvency rules, and defined in the Companies Act 1989 Part 1), health and safety monitoring records for individual employees who have been exposed to hazardous substances (40 years after the last entry under the Control of Substances Hazardous to Health (COSHH) Regulations, 2002) and invoice payments (6 years after the current financial year under the VAT Act, 1994). The implicit need to manage records retention is found, for example, in legislation which relates to the rights and requirements to disclose or provide information to individuals or organisations. This includes freedom of information, data pro-tection and audit, all of which have implications for managing records to ensure they can be found and made available.

Certain laws and regulations apply to all organisations, for instance, those governing finance, tax, employment and health and safety. In addition, there are then sector specific ones, such as the Public Records Act (1958, 1967) for central government. Identifying relevant legislation, regulations and other guidelines can be difficult and time consuming, but a number of publications are available to help (e.g. Retention Guidelines for Local Authorities, RMS, 2003; Fellowes, 2003; Hamer, 2004; Parker, 2003). Your organisation's legal depart-ment should also be able to provide advice.

The consequences for failing to comply with the law or sector regulations may be more or less serious depending on the status of the requirements and the nature of the environ-ment in which the business operates. For example, failure to comply with the recordkeeping requirements of the Data

Protection or Freedom of Information Acts may result in prosecution by the Information Commissioner and a fine.

In addition to ensuring that your organisation provides evidence of its actions, for governance and accountability purposes, two other issues are important in the context of legal and regulatory compliance. These are *admissibility* and *discovery*.

4.1.2 Legal admissibility of electronic records

In the past courts of law in the UK, and in other countries whose legal system is based on the English one, normally considered all records to be *hearsay* evidence, i.e. secondary evidence not given directly by a witness in person, and potentially not admissible as legal evidence. But today, with the passing of legislation such as the Civil Evidence Act (1995) in the UK and the establishment of precedent, records, including electronic records, are like other evidence legally admissible. This means that a court will accept records as part of the evidence, read and consider them; but there is no guarantee that the court will pay any attention to them. The judge may decide they have little *weight*, i.e. little value as evidence.

To reduce the risk of them not having weight, records need to have all the characteristics of 'good' records, discussed in Chapter 2, i.e. authenticity, reliability and integrity. They do not need to be perfect, but the chance of a court (judge) taking notice of them, as valuable evidence, needs to be maximized.

Records will have more weight if:

- they have been created and captured as close as possible in time to the event or transaction to which they relate (e.g. minutes written within hours or days, rather than weeks or months, of a meeting)
- the systems in which they are managed are well-documented and operated, to show that they are used in a consistent manner

and

- where records have been converted from one format or medium to another, best practice guidelines have been followed to make the conversion
- copies, where originals are unavailable, have been appropriately authenticated.

The use of computers and other forms of information and communication technology to create and store records in electronic format has led to much discussion about the admissibility of electronic records in a court of law. There is obvious concern about the ability to change electronic records more easily than paper records without leaving any trace, which emphasizes the importance of well-documented systems which are operated by skilled people. But electronic records are generally admissible as evidence; in fact the objective of the UNCITRAL model laws on e-commerce are

> "to ensure equality of treatment for users of paper documents and of electronic forms of communication."
> (Law Commission, 2001)

And the Electronic Communications Act was the first piece of legislation to confirm the legal recognition of electronic signatures (Electronic Communications Act, 2000). Like other records it is their weight that will determine their value as evidence.

The nature or quality of records and records systems are both very important in litigation whether in defence or prosecution and, in many countries, standards and guidelines are available which, if followed, should ensure the legal admissibility and evidential weight of your organisation's records (e.g. PD 0016 (2001), BIP 0008-1 (2004) and BS 6498 (2002)).

4.1.3 Legal discovery

In any litigation where records are used as evidence to support a case, either by the claimant or the defendant, it is important to be aware that it is usually necessary to disclose *all* the relevant records to the other side. Some of the records may help the case and others may be damaging, but they must all be disclosed. The term used to describe this process is *discovery*.

This does not imply that all records must be kept forever, but it is obviously very important that, when records are destroyed, the action is done to an agreed schedule using standard procedures. If an organisation is seen to be destroying records in an ad hoc manner, then its conduct may be brought into question and it might be accused of covering up the truth, as in the Enron case. This includes the late destruction of records that could and should have been legitimately destroyed sooner, when it has not happened as part of agreed policy and practice.

Conversely, it would be foolish to destroy records which have reached their due destruction date where they might form part of ongoing litigation and, in fact, legal counsel are likely to advise or demand that they be retained until after the proceedings have been completed.

One of the particular challenges of managing legal discovery in the electronic environment is caused by the proliferation of copies, including those retained on back-up tapes and other media. It is relatively straightforward for discovery agents (IT experts) to search and retrieve apparently 'deleted' records. The risk of this occurring needs to be managed and risk management is covered in the next chapter.

4.2 Laws, standards and regulations

This section provides a very brief overview of the record-keeping implications of some of the key common pieces of legislation, regulations and standards using examples from the UK jurisdiction. It is not meant to be comprehensive merely illustrative and indicative of the types of requirements that exist.

4.2.1 Freedom of Information, Data Protection and Human Rights Acts

The Data Protection Act 1998 (DPA) and Human Rights Act (1998) (HRA) apply to all organisations in the UK and the Freedom of Information Act 2000 (FoIA) to all public sector bodies in the UK, although the latter also has implications for the private sector where, for example, public-private partnerships exist.

The first is concerned with an individual's right to privacy and protects that right by preventing inappropriate disclosure of information about them. The second is concerned with a much broader range of individual rights, including privacy, and the third is about openness, transparency and greater accountability of government and public bodies in the pursuit of better democracy.

The DPA establishes a framework for processing (i.e. obtaining, recording, retaining, using and disclosing) personal data about living individuals. This data can be held within both electronic and manual filing systems that enable the individual to be easily identified and the information readily accessed. Critical recordkeeping implications include:

- maintaining the accuracy and currency of the information held
- using the information for the *specified* purposes only, unless the individual has granted permission for their data to be used for other purposes (hence, the question at the bottom of many forms asking for such permission to use for other purposes such as marketing) and
- retaining the data no longer than is necessary for the purpose(s) specified (Principle 5) which requires a records retention schedule that is adhered to by all staff, and
- keeping the information secure (Principle 7) which may require locked cabinets and doors, password protection, clear desk policies and procedures for wiping electronic storage media.

For many organisations Article 8 of the HRA, concerning the right to respect for private and family life, contains the key recordkeeping implications. Since this essentially relates to confidentiality, then compliance with the DPA, and adherence to common law practice of maintaining confidentiality, should ensure compliance with the HRA from a record-keeping perspective.

The FoIA gives members of the public the general right of access to a wide range of information, not just personal data, held by public authorities such as local and central government, the police, schools, colleges and universities and hospitals. Some information may be classed as 'exempt' and not be disclosed, for example information relating to national security and commercial interests, as well as information provided in confidence. However, exemptions are not applied 'automatically' to all information in these categories − rules and tests are applied. Members of the public have had access to a lot of information from various public bodies for a long time. The key points about the FoIA are that some information will be *routinely* available and other information will be accessible in response to an individual (written) request, to which a response must be made within 20 working days.

The major recordkeeping implications for public authorities are the need to:

- have an integrated or co-ordinated approach to information and records management with clearly defined and assigned responsibilities for implementing records management
- have audited their current records management practices to determine what, if anything, is required to comply with the code
- ensure adequate resources are available for managing records
- have a policy statement on how records are managed
- ensure staff are aware of the records management policy and procedures and have or acquire the necessary knowledge and skills to implement it

- put in place effective, well structured recordkeeping systems for ease of identification and retrieval of information and to meet business needs and comply with legal requirements

as identified in the model action plans developed by The National Archives to assist public authorities in achieving compliance with the Lord Chancellor's Code of Practice on managing records under Section 46 of FoIA (The National Archives www.nationalarchives.gov.uk).

Authoritative sources of further information about these acts can be found at the Department for Constitutional Affairs website www.dca.gov.uk, the Information Commissioner's website www.informationcommissioner.gov.uk, the Office of the Scottish Information Commissioner (www.itspublicknowledge.info/) and the JISC Legal Information Service (www.jisc.ac.uk/legal).

4.2.2 Electronic Communications and Regulation of Investigatory Powers Acts

The Electronic Communications Act (2000) (ECA) is concerned with supporting safe e-commerce by facilitating the use of electronic communications and electronic data storage. This is achieved primarily by the legal recognition of digital signatures and providing a registration or approval scheme for cryptography service providers.

Section 7 of the Act "allows an electronic signature, or its certification, to be admissible as evidence in respect of any question regarding the authenticity or integrity of an electronic communication or data" (Electronic Communications Act, 2000). In other words an electronic signature is admissible under the rules of court procedure in the UK and the court will decide what weight should be given to it.

The Regulation of Investigatory Powers Act (2000) (RIPA) is the law which regulates cyberspace by ensuring that "relevant investigatory powers are used in accordance with human rights". These cover the interception of postal and telecommunications, the acquisition of communications data, such as telephone

67

billing records, the interception of user logs and emails of suspected criminals by security and/or intelligence services and access to encrypted data. It also covers the recording of telephone calls.

Both Acts have recordkeeping implications for particular types of organisations, for example digital signature service providers in the case of the ECA and call centres, potentially, in the case of RIPA. But there are implications for all organisations, be it in the way they record and manage the transactions of e-business, storing data and records electronically for evidential purposes, or the way they monitor the use of email.

4.2.3 The Environmental Information Regulations

Whereas the FoIA gives the public the right of access to a wide range of information, the Environmental Information Regulations 2004 (EIR), as the name suggests, concerns the right of access to environmental information. Environmental information is defined very broadly and encompasses, for instance, information about the air, emissions, waste, GM crop trials and pesticide testing. There are a number of differences between the EIR and FoIA but one is the range of organisations to which EIR applies – this includes public utilities, and certain public private partnerships and private companies, for instance in the waste and transport sectors. The implications for good records management, however, are similar to those of the FoIA. Under the EIR organisations will need to handle information requests, be able to locate and disclose environmental information, and in a proactive manner, ensuring third party rights are considered. (Defra, www.defra.gov.uk/corporate/opengov/eir/index.htm).

4.2.4 Sector specific requirements

Some functions common to all organisations, such as employment and health and safety, are covered by regulations and/or legislation which contain specific recordkeeping requirements. In addition, some sectors operate within particular regulations which make further demands on recordkeeping, as indicated earlier (see 4.1.1). Examples within the United Kingdom include:

- charitable organisations which operate under the Charities Act (1993)
- the health sector where Health Circular HSC 1999/053 covers the management of records in National Health Service Trusts and health authorities. It is to be replaced in 2006 by the *Records Management: NHS Code of Practice* (Department of Health, www.dh.gov.uk/assetRoot/04/11/40/95/04114095.pdf)

The pharmaceuticals sector is very heavily regulated and, for example, must adhere to the records requirements within the European GxP regulations (Good Laboratory Practice, Good Clinical Practice and Good Manufacturing Practice legislation) and SI 2005/2789, which has revised existing provisions in UK legislation that implement European Directives on the manufacture of medicinal products. (The MHRA and European Commission websites provide overviews and updates on relevant legislation for the sector). And within the private sector generally all organisations that are listed on the US stock exchange must comply with the Sarbanes-Oxley Act (2002). Although the purpose of this legislation is to improve the integrity of financial auditing and the reliability of resultant audit reports, it does have some recordkeeping requirements. Specifically, companies must have policies, procedures and practices for the management and retention of financial records including those relevant to audit or investigation. The Act prohibits destruction of records which might provide evidence in such situations and outlines the penalties of non-compliance (Stephens, 2005).

4.2.5 National and International standards

In addition to sector specific and generic legislation there are other tools which, whilst not having the 'weight' of the law, have the 'merit' of best practice making them difficult to ignore. These are standards, guidelines and codes of practice for managing records.

In addition to ISO 15489 Parts 1 and 2 (2001) discussed in Chapter 3, there are many standards which address specific aspects of managing records. For example: ISO 18925 (2002) is concerned with the storage of information on optical discs, BS 5454 (2000) with the storage of archival documents, ISO 19005-1 (2005) with the long-term preservation of PDF files, ISO 23081-1 (2006) with metadata for records and ISO/IEC 17799 (2000) with information security.

Guidelines already mentioned include those for implementing ISO 15489, i.e. BIP 0025 Parts 1-3 (2003); PD 5000 (2002) for electronic documents and e-business transactions; BIP 0008 (2004) a code of practice for the legal admissibility and evidential weight of electronically stored information (previously known as PD 0008, 1999) and the associated compliance workbook BIP 0009 (2004), as well as PD0017 (2001) on the preparation of business documents.

4.2.6 Further sources of information

Keeping abreast of changes in legislation, regulations and guidelines is very important, but can be time consuming. Good sources of further information are:

- colleagues in your own organisation, for example lawyers and key individuals in other departments such as personnel, health and safety, finance and quality, who keep up-to-date with issues affecting their own areas
- records management colleagues/peers
- professional associations and societies
- listservs
- national archives guidelines.

Contact details for some of these are given in the appendices at the end.

To assess your organisation's situation in respect of managing records for legal and regulatory compliance complete the Chapter 4 checklist in Appendix A.

Chapter 5

Risk management and business continuity

All organisations share the basic and fundamental goal of staying in business. Their records play a central role in ensuring that this business continuity happens, a point already highlighted as a key priority in Chapter 3. All the more reason, therefore, to protect your records so as to ensure they are available to fulfil the key purpose of supporting business operations.

However, the situation in which organisations operate, whether from an economic, social or political perspective, is at best inhospitable and at worst dangerous. On the one hand your organisation wants to maintain its market position against competitors, but, on the other hand, you are faced by the dangers of terrorism, climate change and anti-social and criminal behaviour. And your records, especially those in electronic format, are inherently complex and challenging to manage because they are only accessible via technology.

An example of the difficulties related to technology is the high profile case of the Domesday Project, referred to in Chapter 3. In this case a resource intensive, expensive and just-in-time rescue operation was necessary to save the data collected in the form of a videodisc by the BBC to celebrate the 900th anniversary of the Domesday Book, while the original remains readable to this day (Darlington, Finney and Pearce, 2003). Also, in the past, when mainframe systems were the norm, technology was centrally managed but now, in the world of the personal computer, both the technology and records are highly distributed and more difficult to manage.

In addition, records in other formats, such as paper, are vulnerable in different ways; for instance risk from water damage through flood or humidity. And there are those records, in a variety of formats, which are vital to the continuing operation of the organisation in the aftermath of a disaster. These *vital* records, as they are called, need special treatment because managing them effectively can make the difference between your organisation being able to operate immediately, surviving or folding after a disaster. The offices of Norton Rose, one of the top ten UK law firms, were damaged in the Bishopsgate bombing in the City of London in 1993. Their servers survived the explosion, but staff were not able to get to their offices because the surrounding buildings were dangerous. They were, however, able to set up operations in the offices of another law firm, to get workstations from their PC suppliers and so very quickly get back into business. (Christian, 2001) More recently, Northgate Information Solutions, a leading supplier of payroll support systems to organisations such as the Police in the UK, lost its building in the oil depot fire at Buncefield, Hemel Hempstead. The fire broke out in the early hours of Sunday 11 December 2005 but the company had a well rehearsed and comprehensive contingency plan including backup procedures for systems data. This meant that a full systems backup had been completed on Friday 9 December and the backups had been sent offsite. Only operational data from the following day was lost because, whilst it had been backed up, it had not been relocated offsite by the time of the explosion on Sunday morning. As a result Northgate were able to continue normal business for their customers very quickly, although the cost of the disruption and the building and facilities lost will be huge. (BBC, 2005)

So the nature of the world today and of the records on which your organisation relies means that there are a lot of potential risks which threaten your business operations. Business continuity should be firmly and explicitly on your business agenda. It requires a systematic approach to understanding and addressing the risks and threats your organisation faces to its routine operations and to exceptional circumstances. And, as it is impossible to anticipate all future events, you need to be prepared in case a threat materialises and a disaster happens.

The theory and practice of risk management provides you with a framework of issues to address and a step-by-step approach to providing solutions. In this guide where the focus is on records, we will concentrate on risk management as it relates to your organisation's records, while not losing sight of the wider organisational context in terms of risk and business continuity.

5.1 Risk management

Risk management involves making decisions about the risks which threaten your organisation's records and acting upon these decisions. The process of risk management involves four elements:

1. risk identification
2. risk analysis
3. responding to risks
4. disaster management and recovery.

The first three provide a methodology in the form of a series of steps to follow. Disaster management and recovery is a separate but related process which prepares your organisation to deal with a disaster and its aftermath. We begin by working through the step-by-step methodology.

5.1.1 Risk identification

The first step is to identify the risks. In general terms a risk, as defined in *Digitising History* (History Data Services, 1999), is

"the chance of exposure to the adverse consequences of future events."

So, the risk identification begins with establishing what the threats are. The threats to records, irrespective of their format, can be categorised into three groups:

1. natural, such as flood, storms, infestation, fire
2. accidental, for example, carelessness, ignorance, mistakes, negligence
3. intentional/deliberate, such as sabotage, theft, terrorism.

It is interesting to note that both the second and third groups are man–made threats, highlighting the importance of the records users, whose roles and responsibilities we explored in Chapter 3.

Considering first *natural* threats it is often common practice to store paper records in basements where, if the building is located near to a river or if the water table is high, they will be vulnerable to floods. In August 2002 severe unseasonal flooding in Prague resulted in loss and damage to archives and other collections (Rogers, 2003).

The electronic environment is particularly prone to *man–made* threats, whether accidental or deliberate. The following two cases demonstrate the point:

- In terms of *deliberate* threats the Enron case springs to mind, but, in fact, because the destruction was not done expertly, discovery experts were still able to get access to the records (Festa and Bowman, 2002).
- The *accidental* threat of not knowing what was required resulted in SG Cowen Securities, a New York based brokerage, having to pay a fine of $100,000 because, although they kept back-up tapes of emails in case of system failure, they did not keep them for the three years required by law (Gerr, 2003).

The different groups of threats then translate into the risks to which records are exposed. The National Archives of Australia (2003) provide a comprehensive list of the kinds of risks which prevail in the electronic environment as follows:

- uncontrolled accumulation of records, documents and data;
- inadvertent destruction of records, documents and data;
- unauthorised tampering with records and documents;
- lack of or absence of systems documentation and associated metadata
- system paralysis or at the very least hindrance in accessing information;
- additional costs associated with the purchase of additional storage;
- increased risk of wholesale, unsystematic and possibly illegal destruction;
- loss of valuable business and archival records;
- increased risk of security breaches;
- unauthorised alteration or deletion of records (loss of evidence);
- public embarrassment;
- unnecessary delays in or breakdowns in the business process; and
- lack of public accountability.

To this list O'Shea (1996) adds

> "poor uncoordinated recordkeeping and duplication caused by the maintenance of parallel paper and electronic systems."

It is important to note at this point that the risks are both physical, i.e. destruction or deletion of records, but also intangible, such as loss of credibility or negative publicity.

The next stage is to analyse the threats and risks and assess how they will affect your organisation.

5.1.2 Risk analysis

The two key steps to risk analysis are to:

1. determine the likelihood of the threat and its associated risk or risks materialising, and then

2. quantify what the impact of the risk will be to the running of your business.

A simple way to do the risk analysis is to use a scale from one to ten for each of the threats/risks identified and their impact, then multiply the values together and so produce a list showing the relative importance of the different risks. The scale for likelihood would use the following values:

1 = very unlikely to happen, for example, the threat of a volcanic eruption in London
5 = likely to happen, for example, incorrect data entry
10 = certain to happen at some time, for example, power failure.

For business impact the values would be:

1 = no effect
5 = disruption to business operation
10 = organisation goes out of business.

So, for an organisation based in London, the threat of a volcanic eruption is unlikely (i.e. a value of 1) but, if it were to happen, it would put the organisation out of business (i.e. a value of 10). This gives a risk value of 10 (i.e. 1 x 10) compared to a value of 25 (i.e. 5 x 5) for incorrect data entry (value 5) which would disrupt the business (also value 5). So the resulting risk analysis would produce a list of risks with values between one and 100, showing the most serious threats or risks and what level of priority might be given to each in managing the risk. From this list decisions can then be made in terms of how to respond.

Victoria Electronic Records Strategy (2003) proposes a slightly different approach, which assesses the likely consequences and rates the risk as either high, medium or low. And Minnesota Historical Society, focusing on legal risk, uses a scale from low risk to high risk for a series of eight key questions relating to records and recordkeeping practices. They also helpfully provide a series of records management scenarios for risk analysis purposes and also provide guidance on possible risk mitigation (Minnesota Historical Society, 2002).

Before the appropriate action of risk mitigation can be decided, there is another element to consider and this relates to cost. The objective is to factor into the risk response an analysis of the cost benefit. In other words, can the response be justified in cost terms? The response should cost less than the costs that would be incurred if the threat/risk materialised.

It is perfectly feasible that, having done the risk analysis and assessment, the decision is to accept the risk. A company may have decided to accept the risk of not keeping email tapes for the required retention period, having calculated that a potential fine would be much less than it would have cost to keep the email tapes for the time stated. Another firm might take the opposite decision, fearing that an adverse court ruling may cost them a lot more in lost reputation.

This raises a very important point about risk analysis and assessment, which is that threats/risks change and therefore it is necessary on a regular basis to review and monitor your risk analysis and assessment, as well as your risk response.

5.1.3 Responding to risks

Having identified and assessed the threats and risks, the final step of the routine process is to decide what response to make to the risk, not forgetting the cost benefit equation.

There are traditionally four responses to threats/risks in general and they can be applied to the management of risks. The possible responses are:

1. terminate
2. treat
3. tolerate
4. transfer.

Terminating a risk would be considered for major or terminal disruption to business activities. For example, in the financial sector, the total dependence on technology to monitor the money markets and access customer records has driven banks and building societies to invest, at great expense, in duplicate hot sites with a fully updated and online system, which can be called into action if the main system fails. This response involves high capital and ongoing costs, but the solution is cost effective because, without this backup, the organisation would not be able to transact business.

For risks which would temporarily or for a short time interrupt business, the response is more likely to be *treatment*. For example, organisations often have reciprocal arrangements for backup of part of their systems. So two universities in neighbouring cities might agree to provide backup of each other's staff payroll systems. This arrangement would only be required at a particular time in the month and would probably not be given high priority.

Tolerating risks, i.e. recognising that the threats/risks exist but not doing anything to mitigate them, may seem an unacceptable response, but may be the only one that your organisation can afford. The risk analysis, however, will have alerted you to the potential threat and risks. So, if the threat does materialise, you will be aware of its potential impact, so can at least monitor its effect and perhaps take some emergency action as part of your disaster recovery procedures. For example, if the roof of your records centre leaks and you cannot afford to repair it, each time it rains you could check to see if any damage has been caused to the records.

The fourth possible response is to *transfer* the risk, which usually means insuring against it. This response, in fact, does not mitigate the risk, but it potentially provides compensation. In the case of records the transfer response has potentially little benefit because the records are unique. For example, in the event of a terrorist act or a natural disaster, it would be possible to get compensation for new workstations but that would not cover the actual records themselves.

Now a fifth response has been added – *train*. This is particularly important when we consider that two categories of threat and many of the risks are dependent on people.

So, in summary, we can say that the response to the threat must be commensurate with, on the one hand, the likelihood of it occurring and its impact on the business and, on the other, with its cost effectiveness. This whole process of risk management of records further reinforces the close relationship between business operations and records.

5.1.4 Disaster management and recovery

The process of risk management for records and recordkeeping is formal and planned. It allows your organisation to assess and address the vulnerability of your records. However, it is never possible to anticipate all of the future events that might affect your records. For example, no-one foresaw the scale of the terrorist attack that hit the Twin Towers in New York on 11 September 2001.

It is therefore necessary to complement risk management with disaster management and recovery. This involves being prepared for a disaster and having in place a plan to recover from its effects. There are some powerful statistics relating to disaster management as follows:

- of the 452 businesses hit by the 1996 bomb in central Manchester, 250 were out of business within six months
- 40% of the businesses affected by the bombing of the World Trade Center in 1993 were bankrupt within two years (Terror in the US: London shocked but prepared, 2001).

So what does disaster management involve? It means having a plan and testing it and it means setting up a team of people and training staff so that they can respond in the event of a disaster. It involves making preparations for alternative working locations, setting up arrangements for storage and protection, particularly of paper documents. For example, freeze-drying wet paper records buys time, by preventing deterioration from mould. This may mean having a standing arrangement with your local freezer company.

For major recovery operations it may be necessary to bring in one of a number of specialist companies, such as Document SOS, which has notably recovered documents from such major disasters as the Piper Alpha oil platform fire in 1988 and 11 September 2001.

5.2 Business continuity

Although we have already spoken of the drive for business continuity at the beginning of this chapter, we want to return to the concept here in conclusion. In the paper world, the response to risk management was the responsibility of few people, often those who managed centralised records centres. Responses tended to focus more on disaster management and recovery. In the e-environment, with its highly distributed arrangement and the reliance on hardware and software systems to get access to records, it is essential to be proactive in ensuring, not only that records are created and captured appropriately, but that they also remain available and are protected as quality records for as long as they are needed.

The emphasis has therefore shifted from the records and their physical protection to ongoing support for the business functions with which they are associated and the systems in which they are kept. And this shift has been reinforced by the Turnbull Report (1999) which requires all publicly listed companies to have a risk management strategy.

So, business continuity, with its two elements of proactive risk management combined with disaster management and recovery, has become the norm, and needs to remain the norm. Risk management and planning for business continuity need to be a continuous process which is integral to the decision-making process within your organisation.

To assess how well your organisation manages risk and is prepared for a potential disaster complete the Chapter 5 checklist in Appendix A.

Chapter 6

Scheduling Records for Retention

6.1 The lynchpin of records management?

Scheduling records for retention means deciding what records need to be kept, for how long, why, where and how. In the world of paper records, managing retention and disposal was often the starting point of a records management programme because the outcome was a reduction in the volume of paper stored, making a visible impact and leading to immediate space and/or cost savings.

Retention management is still an important part of managing records in the e-environment, which is not yet paperless, because it:

- ensures all necessary records are captured and retained for as long as they are needed and no longer
- supports consistent practice across the entire organisation
- encourages timely physical relocation of material from costly office space or e-material from virtual space to less expensive and/or more efficient storage space
- identifies records of long term value, as early as possible, to plan for their preservation and secure them from accidental destruction.

Whilst it may not result in the same visual impact in the e-environment, retention management will ensure that an organisation:

- meets its legal obligations to retain records as evidence of its business activities
- can demonstrate accountability
- protects its own interests in the case of litigation, and
- operates effectively through efficient access to and use of its corporate memory.

6.2 Retention or disposal schedules

A retention schedule, alternatively called a disposal schedule or authority, or retention and disposal schedule, identifies an organisation's records and documents the decisions about how long they are to be kept and why. The decisions must have been formally approved at an appropriate senior level to ensure the schedule has the necessary internal status, to enforce its implementation and to add weight to the organisation's procedures for managing records retention. The schedule is a record itself.

In the e-environment retention decisions can be captured in a number of different ways resulting in different formats of retention schedule, normally:

- a standalone retention schedule
- as metadata incorporated or 'embedded' into an electronic document and records management system (EDRMS), and/or
- as metadata incorporated or 'embedded' into other electronic recordkeeping or business systems/applications.

The nature of a standalone schedule can range from a simple word-processed document or spreadsheet, distributed in hard copy or electronic form, to a database or web-based document published on an organisation's intranet. The format should be fit-for-purpose and will depend on the organisational needs and the resources available to develop and maintain it.

The benefit of a standalone schedule is that it acts as a dissemination mechanism. It prompts action, helping staff to know what records they need to keep and what they should destroy when and how. It highlights their responsibilities and gives them confidence to act appropriately.

Where the schedule is incorporated into an e-recordkeeping system of some kind, the retention decisions must still have been approved. This means the schedule should be captured either in a module or part of the system, in a way that allows it to be managed as a record, or captured as a separate record, like the standalone retention schedule. The benefit of incorporating retention metadata into e-systems is that elements of retention management can be automatically managed, for example automatic prompting for deletion and deletion itself, in certain circumstances.

In reality the current hybrid nature of the e-environment means that different formats of retention schedule may be needed for different purposes. All formats should be accompanied by user guidelines to ensure correct implementation. And, in the case of schedules embedded in an EDRMS or other e-recordkeeping system/application, a simple explanation of how retention is managed in those systems will be required, together with procedures for capturing records into the systems and identifying which documents should be destroyed.

6.3 Developing a retention schedule

The traditional approach to scheduling records has been to conduct a survey or audit of what records an organisation has, decide how long they should be kept, why and where, create a retention schedule to document those decisions and then implement it. This 'bottom up' approach, so-called because of its focus on what records the organisation has, has worked reasonably well in the paper environment where records collections are easily seen and understood. But it has its limitations. For instance it is not always easy to identify gaps in the creation and/or capture of records or local differences in naming similar types or classes of records series, e.g. project reports versus study reports; and it can be very time consuming to conduct physical audits or surveys using questionnaires and/or interviews.

This approach may still be practical for very small organisations, with stable structures and business goals, and for scheduling legacy records collections. But in today's e-environment the volume of records and their virtual nature make this approach potentially very difficult, so organisations are turning to the functional or business activity approach to scheduling.

6.3.1 Functional or business activity approach

The functional approach is based on the premise that records are the inputs to and outputs of business functions and activities. It considers what an organisation does and therefore what it should have in terms of records to document its activities, rather than what is has got. This is a 'top down' approach to retention scheduling which focuses on the organisation's business, and identifies:

- the functions that support it in achieving its purpose and conducting its business
- the activities undertaken to fulfil those functions, and
- the transactions which form part of the activities.

The records resulting from transactions provide information about, and evidence of, the organisation's functions and activities.

This is the approach recommended in ISO 15489-1 (2001) and DIRKS (National Archives of Australia, 2001; State Records New South Wales, 2003) and variations on it have been used in practice (Horsman, 1997 and Morelli, 1999).

The advantages of the functional or business activity approach are that:

- gaps, duplication and variations in the management of records are more easily identified and handled

- 'unnecessary' records can be eliminated
- resources can be focused on the records associated with the functions and activities of highest priority, and
- it offers a more pragmatic approach to scheduling electronic records because it does not require a detailed survey of what records already exist.

In many ways the functional approach to retention scheduling lies at the opposite end of the spectrum to the records approach but, in reality, a combination of the two may be the most effective.

6.3.2 Records of common vs. core functions

Some functions and activities are common to all organisations, for example personnel management, finance, health and safety and aspects of administration, as we saw in Chapter 2. Others are core, or special, to the organisation because of the sector in which it operates. For example, teaching for a university, drug discovery and development for a pharmaceuticals company, programme making for a TV company. And for core functions and activities there may be common types of records, such as those relating to meetings or project management.

It makes sense to adopt or adapt published examples of retention schedules for common functions, and common records of core functions, and not reinvent the wheel. National archives, professional societies and large public sector organisations publish schedules of this kind. Examples include:

- The National Archives www.nationalarchives.gov.uk/recordsmanagement/advice/schedules.htm
- State Records New South Wales (2004) Disposing of State Records www.records.nsw.gov.au/publicsector/disposal/disposal.htm
- National Archives of Australia (2000) Administrative functions disposal authorities www.naa.gov.au/recordkeeping/disposal/authorities/GDA/afda/summary.html

It is sometimes possible to find an example that covers a particular sector which can be used as a starting point, for instance, the Local Government Retention Schedule (www.rms-gb.org.uk/resources/91)

Assuming you adopt or adapt schedules for common functions then you can concentrate effort on scheduling the records of your core functions and activities. The starting point is an information collection and analysis exercise.

6.3.3 Collecting information for retention scheduling

In simple terms this process comprises three key steps:

1. understanding your organisation's business and how it is performed, including the key stakeholders who influence how it operates, the risks it faces and its attitude to risk
2. identifying the organisation's functions, activities and transactions and capturing them in a business classification scheme
3. identifying the legal, regulatory, business, best practice and possibly community/societal requirements for creating and keeping records.

This will first involve collecting information from internal documents, such as the mission statement, organisational goals and objectives, organisation charts, business plans and targets, policies, standards etc, supplemented by interviews with appropriate staff. The information will then need to be analysed to map the organisation's functions and activities in the form of a *business classification scheme*. This is usually a hierarchical diagram or view of what the organisation does and how it does it, which maps the relationships between the functions and activities. It will be more or less detailed depending on the organisation's size, complexity and needs (Morelli, 2005). The business classification scheme can be used for a range of purposes, in this case as a functional framework for a retention schedule. Lastly, external documents such as laws, regulations, standards and best practice/industry guidelines will also need to be identified and consulted, to establish what records should be created and kept to provide information about and evidence of each business function, activity and transaction.

An important question to consider is how much information needs to be collected and analysed to develop a retention schedule? Ultimately, it is important to cover all of the organisation's functions, and therefore records, but this may not be feasible in one project or initiative. It is arguably better to identify all of the high-level functions initially and capture the holistic, organisation-wide view in the business classification scheme. Each function can then be addressed at a more detailed level of activities and transactions and added to the scheme.

The level of detail required may vary, according to how business critical a function and its particular activities are, and will be linked to the organisation's approach to risk management. For some business critical activities it may be important to extend the analysis to a mapping of the business processes (see Morelli, 1999).

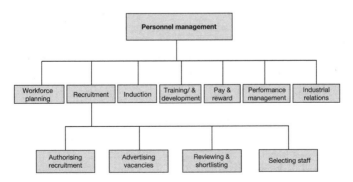

Figure 5 Sample from a business classification scheme showing some of the functions and activities associated with personnel management

6.3.4 Drafting a schedule

A business classification scheme provides the basic structure for a retention schedule. For each activity two other elements need to be added:

- the groups or classes of records, and
- the retention periods or disposal actions.

The following example relating to recruitment activity (see Figure 5 above) illustrates how this can be done.

If the business classification scheme has been developed to a greater level of detail then it will show that part of this activity, selecting staff, involves amongst other things:

- setting the time and place of the interviews and any other tests or presentations which are part of the selection process, and booking the necessary room(s)
- circulating the interview schedule and relevant papers including the short list of applicants, their applications and references (if appropriate), interview note forms etc.

And results in the following types of records being created:

- the interview schedule and short list of applicants
- application forms and references for each applicant
- interview notes
- results of tests and/or presentations (where appropriate)
- final interview report and selection of a suitable candidate(s) for the post(s).

Following on from this there will be:

- rejection letters, and
- an offer letter(s) to the successful applicant(s).

If the functional analysis has not been completed to this level of detail the record types will need to be identified at this point.

Each record type (or series) could be listed individually in a schedule and appropriate retention periods attached. However, some of the records will need to be retained for the same length of time and it will be more manageable if they are grouped together into *classes*. The result is fewer classes of records, comprising related record types. In this example there are three obvious classes, the second needing to be kept longer than the other two:

- the records relating to the administrative arrangements and process of selection
- the offer letter(s) to the successful applicant(s) and related documentation such as the application and references
- records relating to the unsuccessful applicants.

Once this process has been completed for the entire recruitment activity it may be that more records can be added to the first and last classes above and that those two classes can be combined.

Once the classes have been determined each one needs to be given an appropriate title and/or short description. The descriptions should be easy to understand and clearly define what records are included, perhaps using examples. If two classes of records were finally identified for the entire recruitment activity, then they might be described as follows:

- records documenting the filling of vacancies (temporary and permanent) including adverts, applications, references, interview/test reports and letters to unsuccessful applicants
- offer letters to successful applicants and related documentation e.g. application and references. *(See Personnel – Employment)*.

Notice that the records relating to successful applicants then become part of another class relating to their employment. The retention period and/or disposal action can then be added to each class. Deciding how long to keep records is covered in the next section.

A retention schedule may contain other features, for example:

- the authority, regulation or business reason governing the retention
- the official record holder
- a breakdown of the total retention period if the records are to be handled differently at different periods (e.g. where responsibilities, storage medium or even location change)
- method of destruction, e.g. wiping, confidential shredding, recycling
- classification status, e.g. vital
- storage medium and/or format, e.g. electronic (.rtf, .pdf etc), paper, microfilm.

The first two are strongly recommended. The first documents the basis for the decision and both support the schedule's ongoing maintenance. The second supports its implementation, as do the third and fourth. The last two may be captured in something other than a retention schedule, but the final one is particularly important in the e-environment for preservation purposes.

Examples of retention schedules can readily be found on the Web sites of the various national archives already mentioned and of individual organisations. Examples are sometimes found in journal articles and books.

6.3.5 Deciding how long to keep records

Deciding how long to keep records is not always easy and few laws or regulations specify particular periods, preferring instead statements such as 'for as long as the product or test substance is in use'. (Financial regulations are one notable exception with many records needing to be kept for six years beyond the financial year in which they were created). Decisions will need to be determined through the process of appraisal, discussed in Chapter 2, a notoriously difficult aspect of records management.

Different appraisal strategies exist, from the Grigg review-based approach used for more than half a century in the government sector, to the macro functional approach and an approach based on the use, value and users of records (Shepherd and Yeo, 2003: 146-161). Your organisation's appraisal strategy must be based on:

- its need to use records for their information content to support business operations (the corporate memory)
- the need to provide evidence of legal or regulatory compliance and to protect its rights (the evidential memory), and
- potential cultural purposes, where people, usually outside the organisation, will use the records for research and learning (the collective memory).

Inevitably conflicts will arise. In these cases retention decisions should be made on the best advice available, be that the consensus of opinion from knowledgeable people in the organisation or sector best practice, and risk assessment. What are the risks associated with not creating, capturing and/or maintaining the records for as long as required and the risks of keeping records longer than required and available for discovery? They need to be determined and considered.

The total retention period is usually one of the following types:

- a specific period, e.g. 6 years beyond the year they were created, as in the case of many financial transactional records
- a period dependent on an event, e.g. the termination of an agreement plus a specified number of years
- indefinite or permanent, e.g. deeds of incorporation, treaties and others relevant to the particular type of organisation

- review at a later date, e.g. some subject files or even project files.

The last category relates to informational value, which is not intrinsic, and should only be used when it is not possible to predict the likely future importance of the records for the organisation and/or others.

6.3.6 Official records, copies and transitory records

One downside of the e-environment is the proliferation of copies of records. Another is the multiple media existence of some records, although increasingly, there may only be an e-record as no direct paper equivalent of complex, compound, multi-media records from databases, spreadsheets, video broadcasts etc., will exist.

Two questions to ask are:

1. Is the paper version or the electronic version to be the official record?
2. Who is the official record holder?

The answers will determine which are *convenience copies*, or duplicates, and which are the *originals*.

Originals must be managed in accordance with the retention period and/or disposal action in the schedule. Some convenience copies are necessary legitimate working copies, e.g. a manager's copy of his/her annual budget or the minutes of a meeting, but they should not be retained longer than the official record holder's original. They should be disposed of at any time earlier than that. Identifying the official record holder identifies the group with responsibility for the original record and its retention in accordance with the schedule. It also provides a simple strategy for managing the huge volumes of duplicate electronic and paper copies of records.

Other records that may have a very short life include, for example, agendas of meetings which become subsumed within the minutes after the meeting has taken place and some drafts, although some organisations may wish to keep drafts of contracts and other records to ensure they have the full details of a process. These records can be termed *transitory* records and can be managed using the same strategy as for convenience copies.

Instructions for managing copies and transitory records should be incorporated into the retention schedule or be part of any accompanying guidelines. You may be able to stipulate that such records are kept for no longer than one year and provide a list of types of transitory records. It is a simple, pragmatic solution that records creators and users can easily follow and which will help them to help the organisation manage its records, referred to sometimes as normal administrative practice.

6.4 Implementation and maintenance

Before the retention decisions can be implemented they need to be approved, so that the schedule, in whichever form it is captured (see 6.2), has authority. Prior to seeking approval it can be useful to test it. If a purely functional approach is adopted, it may be that some of the details of why and how records are stored and used are missing, or that other legacy records exist and have been missed altogether, and/or not all of the needs for records retention, especially future needs, have been addressed. Sample surveys of some records and/or further discussions with staff may serve to fill these gaps and achieve the best possible analysis for the resource investment available. It is at this point, therefore, that in practice the functional approach sometimes meets the records approach.

Implementation could either be phased, for example by function or department, linked to an office move, current versus retrospective records, or a concentrated effort across the entire organisation, using a 'big bang' approach. Again the decision will depend on the particular circumstances, the size of the task, the resources available, the sense of urgency and the priorities.

Whichever approach is taken, training and awareness will be required to support staff to review records against the schedule and dispose of them (i.e. destroy or relocate) accordingly. It will be important to have agreed a procedure for authorising the destruction of *original* records and approving the destruction process itself, which may include agreed and verified procedures with external service organisations, for instance for confidential shredding. This will create records of destruction, which will need to be included in the schedule. And the schedule, whatever its form, is of course also a record to be managed.

Publishing and implementing the schedule is not the end of the exercise – it will need to be kept up-to-date. A review process will be required to ensure that any legislative or regulatory changes which impact on records retention are incorporated and any decisions based on business needs are still appropriate. If a functional approach has been taken, then the classes of records should be fairly stable, unless there has been a significant change to the organisation's business, for instance through a merger or acquisition.

6.5 Scheduling legacy records

Legacy records, such as collections of old paper records or records of legacy systems, also need to be scheduled. Some may be covered by classes in the schedule and can simply be actioned accordingly. Others may not. Where the records have been identified, then research into the organisation's history may be needed in order to determine appropriate retention decisions. Where records have not been identified, then an audit or survey will be required. This may be reasonably straightforward for physical records but can be time consuming for electronic records. Recommended sources of guidance on conducting surveys of both physical and e-records include The National Archives (www.nationalarchives.gov.uk/recordsmanagement); the DIRKS Manual Appendix 8 Procedures for developing a records disposal authority in the

Commonwealth (National Archives of Australia, 2001); State Records New South Wales retention and disposal authority (2003) and Shepherd and Yeo (2003).

6.6 Summary

Scheduling records for retention is a crucial element of managing your organisation's records, but the process can be time consuming to develop and implement. Therefore, it is important to take a pragmatic approach. This may involve:

- taking decisions about the level of detail captured in the schedule
- managing the risk of retaining records longer or shorter than may be required (which may be related to the level of detail captured)
- adopting a risk assessed strategy for handling legacy records, and/or
- bearing in mind the Pareto rule that 80% of the task will be completed in 20% of the time and the remaining 20% of the task will take the other 80% of your time!

Is having a detailed schedule that has not been approved and implemented any better than having no schedule at all but being able to demonstrate retention management through custom and practice?

To assess your organisation's current management of records retention, complete the Chapter 6 checklist in Appendix A.

Chapter 7

Approaches to managing e-records

In Chapter 3 you were introduced to the different models, a framework, a methodology and the overall records management programme approach. We also explored the range of roles and responsibilities in managing records for the e-environment.

It is clear that technology is central, as:

- a driver
- the underlying infrastructure
- the creating, access and storage medium.

Technology can also offer part of the solution to record-keeping through a range of possible software systems. But we need also to consider how to ensure that recordkeeping becomes a natural, effective and efficient part of business operations. And just as you saw in Chapter 3, it is not a question of one approach fits all. It is all about matching the approach to your organisation, which critically means managing the change in working practices.

So, in this chapter we explore:

- types of software systems for managing records
- procedures for managing e-records over time
- a paradigm shift in the way our electronic desktop system might look
- approaches to integrating electronic recordkeeping into the way business is done in the electronic environment.

7.1 Software systems

In Chapter 2 you saw that standard office software does not by default incorporate recordkeeping functionality. Its whole premise is to allow maximum flexibility in creating and manipulating information for access and re-use with little if any emphasis on the capture of fixed and inviolate electronic objects, which is what we need for electronic recordkeeping. Standard office software does have some potential to be used for recordkeeping, e.g. file properties for capturing metadata and read-only versions of files, but the procedures need to be set up.

There are, however, specialist software products which are specifically designed for managing records. In a guide of this size it is not possible to discuss individual products in detail. We have therefore concentrated on identifying the different types of software for managing electronic records which have paper analogues and pointed you to where you can find more detailed information. You do, however, need to remember that records in the e-environment can exist in the form of sound, video, virtual reality models etc. and these formats continue to evolve and be added to. Adrian Brown (2003) uses the example of the records of the Public Inquiry into the sinking of the MV Derbyshire, which sank in the Pacific in 1980. The records include underwater video, still images, sonar data and a virtual reality model, as well as the more conventional document type records.

The specialist software products for managing records can be divided into three groups:

- file management systems
- electronic document management systems (EDMS)
- electronic records management systems (ERMS) or electronic document and records management systems (EDRMS).

File management systems are really electronic systems for managing records and are used principally for managing paper records, commonly in the non-current phase of the records' life when they are often stored together in a records centre. They are mainly used for tracking file movements and for retention management.

However, a number of the file management systems have now been developed to link to the second group, electronic document management systems (EDMS). As their name implies, their core functionality is not recordkeeping. Rather they focus on information access by providing creation and management controls, such as use of standard templates for different types of documents, audit trails of who created and who has used or changed the document, and version control. It is important to note that EDMS are not a single technology. They comprise powerful information storage and retrieval systems, scanning technology, publication facilities. They often claim to manage the electronic document life cycle, but fall short of full recordkeeping functionality. They do not include retention as standard and treat each file as a separate item rather than in groups based on the business transactions to which they relate. They have, however, made significant impact in both the public and private sectors, because they provide rapid access to an organisation's valuable information resource, and so senior managers have immediately seen their worth and benefit.

The third category comes in two types:

- a software product specifically for recordkeeping, which interfaces with but is separate from other electronic information systems (ERMS)
- a combination of software for recordkeeping and document management (EDRMS).

As their names indicate they provide full recordkeeping functionality in terms of creation, capture, access, and management over time of records in electronic form.

Bob Wiggins (2000) provides a very clear picture of the differences between EDMS and ERMS in the following table:

ERMS	EDMS
Records are pieces of recorded information providing evidence relating to business transactions	**Documents** are coherent units of information meaningful to their relevant users
Administrative control	Operational use
Physical storage	Work flow
File classification	Indexing
Retention	Revision and version control
Statutory and legal requirements	Operational needs
Storage media	Information content
Integrated series	Individual items

The best place to get an authoritative list of ERMS is the records management section of The National Archives website (National Archives www.nationalarchives.gov.uk/ electronicrecords/reqs2002/approved.htm). There you will find the software products which have met the 2002 functional requirements for electronic recordkeeping in government departments. While this requirements specification was designed for government departments, it can apply to any organisation.

7.2 Procedures for managing e-records over time

As well as deciding which software solution you are going to adopt you also need to consider other technology-dependent issues. EDMS, ERMS and EDRMS interface with business software, so, in terms of keeping records for as long as they are needed, there are multiple lives or continua to take into account:

- the lifetime of the record, i.e. the bits and bytes which make up the record

- the lifetime of the storage medium on which the record resides
- the lifetime of the standard office software or other software in which the electronic record was created, and
- the lifetime of the EDMS/ERMS/EDRMS.

Potentially and typically they will not be for the same periods nor will the various lifetimes align. So, the record might be created two years into the lifetime of the office software, captured into the brand new ERMS, and stored on the hard disk of an aging server from which data is routinely backed up onto a CD-ROM, which might last six months or 20 years.

So, what strategies are available to you to ensure that quality electronic records are available for as long as they are needed, which has to be the bottom line? Additionally what about those electronic records which have to be preserved permanently?

There are basically two workable strategies:

1. emulation
2. migration.

Emulation involves recreating the hardware and software environment in which the electronic file was originally created. So, for example an emulator has been developed for the obsolete BBC computer which allows original BBC software to run on a standard PC. This means that every time a new hardware and software environment is created a new emulator is required. In terms of recordkeeping, emulation "preserves the 'original look and feel' of an electronic record" (Brown, 2003), but it is expensive and labour intensive. It is organisations like The National Archives, with their unique responsibility for preserving the records of government which are likely to have been created in many and varied systems, who might routinely use emulation. In the majority of organisations emulation would tend only to be used for rescue missions of critical legacy systems.

The second strategy, *migration*, involves converting records to new formats when the existing formats are replaced with software upgrades. So, for example, WordPerfect for DOS files can be migrated to Microsoft Word for Windows. There is often some loss of information, for example to do with formatting. The key issue from a recordkeeping point of view is whether the loss will threaten the authenticity of the record. Migration is less expensive and more routine as software developers often build migration paths into their products. There is also a move to use XML technology, a widely supported open standard which separates the content from the way in which it is presented. This gives the option to preserve quality electronic records over time in a software-independent way.

Many people have opted to retain records in PDF format where it is possible to create a PDF version. The problem with this format is that it is 'feature-rich' which can cause problems over time. ISO 19005-1 (2005), referred to as PDF/A the 'A' taken to mean 'archive', specifies how to use a subset of PDF components that is more suitable for archival preservation than full PDF. But, if using the PDF/A approach, it is important also to have policies and procedures to ensure acceptable replication of the source records.

But both emulation and migration require resources and there need to be schedules planned to ensure preservation of and access to electronic records over time. Records in current use would need to be migrated at the point the system is upgraded while those no longer in active use but which are still required will need to be kept.

With both strategies it is essential to know how long the records need to be available and what type of availability is required over time. It is unlikely to be necessary to keep financial records online for the whole seven year period that they should be retained. If, however, the financial records system is changed, it is likely that the records of the previous year would need to be migrated because they will be subject to audit. If the records do not need to be consulted in a live system, there is always the option to download the records to paper. All of these decisions are determined by the nature of the records and how they are used, but with the additional requirement to factor in the lifetime of the recordkeeping system.

There is also a further lifetime to consider and that is the longevity of the medium on which the electronic records are stored. The storage media, whether magnetic in the form of tape or disks or magneto-optical or optical in the form of CD-ROMs or optical disks, do deteriorate over time. But even if they are protected in environmentally controlled conditions, there is no guarantee that there will be hardware to read them into the future. We probably all have well preserved 5.25 inch diskettes without the means to read them.

These strategies for digital preservation rely on having access to technical documentation manuals for hardware, software, operating systems and file formats. Like the retention schedule these manuals become important records in their own right and your organisations should be managing them as part of your recordkeeping activities. The National Archives have established the PRONOM system which 'is a web-enabled database of information about software products and file formats [including] information about who developed and supports a product, when it was released, when support will cease, the minimal technical requirements, and the file formats that it can read and write' (Brown, 2003). This could potentially be of benefit to your organisation if you need to migrate legacy systems for which you no longer have the relevant documentation.

7.3 John McDonald's vision

Understanding the lifetimes of the system and storage media in relation to how records are managed and preserved needs to be an important aspect of managing electronic records. The multiple lives/continua add complexity, but the technology brings flexibility and the possibility of new ways of approaching the management of electronic records.

The majority of organisations today use Microsoft Office products which provide a range of content free software for managing text, numbers, structured data, web pages and pre-sentations. You, as the end-user, choose the standard software relevant to the task in hand, for example word-processing for a report, spreadsheet for a budget, database for customer information. But if you are producing your annual report, the chances are that you will need to use all three pieces of soft-ware. So, John McDonald back in 1995 suggested that, instead of being presented with these standard software options, you should have a very different set of icons on your PC desktop. Then at the National Archives of Canada, he shared his vision of the modern office of the future, which he likened to taming the wild frontier. He wrote:

> "Right now my screen is full of icons that represent a 'toolbox' of software utilities such as word processing, spreadsheet, e-mail, database, etc. In the future, as a programme manager, I want a screen that contains icons that reflect the business activities that I manage. In my work environment at the National Archives, I want the icons to be based on the Operational Plan Framework (OPF) of the department. When I click on the 'devel-opment' icon, for instance, I want to be provided with a number of options. I may want to initiate a project, monitor it, write a memo on some aspect of it, or perhaps organise a meeting about the project. Rather than develop a project proposal from scratch, I would like to see the appro-priate form already set up using style sheets and macros imported from word processing or project management software. The proposal form would reflect the format and rules that my division has decided upon for devel-oping project proposals. When I click on the routing list for my proposal, rather than having to select from all of the names of the staff in the National Archives, I want to see the names of those people who normally receive 'development' project proposals." (McDonald, 1995)

Basically what John McDonald is saying is that there should be a match between our virtual and business environments where we see more and more automated and integrated business processes. He revisited his vision in 2002 when he presented one of the keynote papers at the RMS annual conference in Cardiff and, most recently, in a 2005 publication (McDonald, 2005). The 'wild frontier is not so wild anymore' because of:

- substantial investment in online government, e-government
- increased intimacy between business process and customer
- employee demand for services the same as those provided to customers.

What is needed is a change in paradigm to reinforce the basic principle that records are integral to business processes. But if there needs to be a change, then it is essential to acknowledge the fact and actively manage the change. Change management has in fact developed into a new discipline and constitutes a body of knowledge which brings together elements from engineering, business and psychology. But the prime focus of change management is people as Hiatt and Creasey (2003) in their definition of change management explain:

> "Change management is the process, tools and techniques to manage the people-side of business change to achieve the required business outcome, and to realize that business change effectively within the social infrastructure of the workplace."

For change to be effected in the workplace you need to address not only the business strategy, processes, systems, organisational structures and job roles, but also the way in which people will embrace and accept the change in question. So what Hiatt and Creasey (2003) call the "traditional values of control, predictability and consistency . . .that made change relatively simple to implement" need, in the electronic environment, to be replaced by the values of empowerment, accountability and ownership. The change needs to happen and be managed over time, a step-by-step harmonisation of the implementation of systems and processes with preparing the people (see Fuzeau, 2005 for an example of such a harmonisation).

7.4 Approaches to integrating electronic recordkeeping into business operations

Having access to the right software for managing records is only part of the solution. And John McDonald and his paradigm have begun to point us in one possible direction. It is all about ensuring that recordkeeping is a routine part of conducting business and with the ICTs (Information and Communication Technologies) you have powerful tools to support you in achieving this goal. The bottom line is:

- understanding your organisation and its recordkeeping requirements
- harnessing the technology appropriately, and
- managing 'the people-side of business change effectively' (Hiatt and Creasey 2003).

The awareness of the need for good recordkeeping in the current business climate, where accountability and transparency are such a high priority, is also growing, not least because of high profile cases where failure to keep good records has resulted in prosecution or disastrous outcomes as highlighted in Chapter 1.

But not one size or one approach fits all. The method adopted will depend on the size, infrastructure and culture of the organisation. So what are the options?

7.4.1 EDRMS or ERMS for whole or part

For a large organisation with key drivers for recordkeeping, for example a large government department, getting the resource to implement an EDRMS across the whole organisation will not be a problem. Alternatively, in a pharmaceutical company or in other types of manufacturing companies which are ISO 9000 accredited, implementing an ERMS for the core records of submitting a drug for approval or of the manufacturing and maintenance processes will again be relatively straightforward to justify and resource. In both of these scenarios there is also likely to be a records manager to direct and monitor recordkeeping operations or at least someone with designated responsibility to which they would devote considerable time.

There may also be a standard approach to project management, for example PRINCE (PRINCE2, 2001), which provides a framework for implementing and monitoring the new system. The software will provide the recordkeeping functionality, but will not supply the retention rules and business classification scheme specific to the organisation implementing the system. Getting the rules and the scheme right are critical to the success of the system and these tasks provide an ideal opportunity to get the users involved.

7.4.2 Embed records management functionality within business processes

Other organisations are embedding records management functionality within business processes. So, for example, in an insurance company using workflow to deal with insurance claims, the records of the process can be managed within the business process. The customer's claim would start the process and at successive stages other records are produced. It is essential that the full range of recordkeeping functionality issues, from creation and capture and especially retention and long term preservation, are incorporated into the system at the design stage. And this brings us closer to John McDonald's vision of a PC desktop which presents icons of the tasks we do. In this scenario the responsibility for recordkeeping often resides with the managers of each of the business units with perhaps in addition a records manager acting as an internal consultant.

In this scenario each business process will need to be analysed to identify the record inputs to and outputs from the activity. This again is an obvious activity in which to involve the users.

Using standard office software

But many organisations, especially small and medium-sized enterprises, would find it difficult to finance an EDRMS or ERMS even for some of their recordkeeping or to embed records management into their business processes. They do, however, have technology at their disposal which they can use to manage their electronic records. There are also best practice guidelines to help in setting up a system to create, capture, maintain and manage records over time, including destruction and long-term preservation. It is unlikely that they will have a records management specialist and the responsibility for recordkeeping often falls to the administrator or finance manager. There will be fewer people involved, which makes it easier from some points of view, but there is no readymade solution.

It is possible to:

- use templates to ensure consistent and appropriate creation
- force the capture of metadata using the File Properties facility in Microsoft Office products
- set up shared drives based on business functions
- standardise naming conventions.

It is also important to:

- make a regular backup copy, for example, weekly copying of all files or selected folders to CDROM and storing it out of the office
- plan ahead to migrate those records which need to be kept active when the system is upgraded.

7.5 Managing the change

These options only work if the people who are involved adopt and adapt to the change. A good way to start to manage change is to begin to change individual practice. Earlier in this chapter we said that it is important that people are empowered and take ownership of their role in recordkeeping. They need to be given the authority to take action. One example would be to manage convenience copies. As indicated in Chapter 6, the first step would be to designate the **official record** and its holder and then allow the destruction of *copies*, made for convenience by individual users, within a fixed maximum period, once the individual no longer requires the copy.

From this one small but potentially very empowering step you can then move on to engaging them in other record-keeping tasks, such as changing the fileplan or directory structure. Gradually, step-by-step this gets your users into new ways of working where they feel ownership and become accountable for recordkeeping in the electronic environment.

To achieve this goal your users need to:

- understand the key principles of recordkeeping
- be provided with practical skills in the form of training, and
- be provided with manuals and other documentation.

Finally, they need to work with colleagues, because recordkeeping in the electronic environment requires effective partnerships between IT, administration and recordkeeping.

Assess your organisation's current approach to managing electronic records retention by completing the Chapter 7 checklist in Appendix A.

Chapter 8

Managing email in practice

Having looked at the principles of managing records in the e-environment and the main approaches, the purpose of this chapter is to consider applying them in the context of a specific practical situation. The example selected is the case of email.

There have been many widely publicised 'email blunders' including:

- the 'good day to bury bad news' email sent by a UK central government department advisor shortly after the terrorist horrors of 11 September, 2001 in America
- the 'clean up your files' email from a US investment banker sent whilst a legal investigation was ongoing
- deletion of emails from the White House email system (PROFs) at the break of the Iran-contra scandal
- the sacking of a UK high street bank employee after emails revealed the employee had been using a significant amount of company time to conduct personal business, and
- the online public display of Enron emails revealing not only business content but private correspondence including names, security numbers and bank details.

As Nancy Flynn puts it, "careless clicks can – and do – sink corporate ships" (Biggest email blunders of 2003). A director of the ePolicy Institute, Flynn points out that such email blunders:

"underscore the need for organisations to establish email policies, educate employees about email risks and rules,

113

and enforce email policies with software" (Biggest email blunders of 2003).

To approach the email management challenge we begin by asking some key questions, then consider the main options for managing email and provide some solutions within the context of three fictitious scenarios. Together they should provide the full spectrum of likely situations for most organisations, so that you can adapt or adopt a strategy for your organisation.

8.1 Key questions

Question 1. What is email?

Email is an electronic postal system and a communication system.

Question 2: What has email got to do with records?

Initially, email was used to deliver records, in the form of attachments. Today, however, email is considered by many to be the business communication system par excellence and is used to support business operations and decision-making. Therefore the email message *is* the record.

But are all emails records? No. Emails are only records if they have a business context and relate to a business activity. So, the 'let's meet for lunch' type of email relates to a personal activity, has no business context and therefore, strictly, is not a business record. An organisation may, however, consider them to be records, as they could, for instance, provide evidence of contravention of their email usage policy. Emails that are records are those where:

- business is being transacted (between two or more parties) and both/all parties are involved, or

- the originating activity results in disseminating a record for information leading to action, in which case the originator is the record holder, or
- the activity relates to business, but is transitory (e.g. arranging a meeting).

Question 3. What is the problem/challenge with email?

Emails present the following challenges or problems:

1. huge volume
2. variety of items
   2.1. emails are as varied as paper postal communications
   2.2. they are *not* a single record series
3. variety of aspects
   3.1. highly individual and therefore personal activity
   3.2. used for business
   3.3. used for personal communications.

Given the nature of email and the fact that many emails today are records, and are different types of records, how can they be managed?

8.2 Options

No matter which approach is taken (see below), managing email requires:

- a policy with clearly identified roles and responsibilities
- guidelines which provide practical advice on what to do
- a system for managing those email messages which are records.

An email policy must cover both:

- acceptable use, and
- recordkeeping.

Many organisations' email policies cover the former but not the latter.

Acceptable use covers:

- what an organisational email system can be used for – only business purposes or some limited personal use
- when to use email
- how to write emails
- privacy, confidentiality and ethics
- responsibilities and accountability.

In one publicised email blunder, where the content of an email caused the organisation severe embarrassment, the company considered providing every employee with a separate email account (e.g. a Yahoo or Hotmail account) for personal use and restricting use of the business email system for business purposes only.

An email policy which also covers recordkeeping, on the other hand, would include:

- identification of email records
- naming conventions, filing and maintenance – when, where and how to capture them
- email threads and attachments
- copies
- retention
- security and encryption
- preservation, and
- responsibilities.

Guidelines are usually separated from the policy because they are more detailed and more likely to change, for instance when the details of a system or contact point changes. They should tell staff what to do with emails that are records as well as those which are not. In the case of emails that are records the guidelines should detail the system for managing them and what staff must do to operate it. In the case of emails that are not records then the guidelines may take the form of tips and recommended good practice.

What systems options are there? Currently the three main options are to:

1. manage emails within the email system and/or the e-office environment
2. use an EDMS, or
3. use an EDRMS.

Option 1 involves using individual and shared folders to organise emails, deleting emails (manually and perhaps automatically, as in emails which are removed from the wastebasket) and using archiving facilities/functionality but with care. (Many suppliers promote archiving functionality or bolt-on systems as the solution to email management, but mostly they simply remove emails from the current folders to some offline or near-line location – a potential 'dumping ground', rich for discovery, rather than a records management solution. Archiving should not of course mean this). Where additional functionality from the office environment is employed, such as using the *Save As* facility in Microsoft Outlook and then storing the saved item in a shared directory structure, this can support recordkeeping.

Option 2, using an EDMS, means that emails will be managed well as information carriers, with version control and good search and retrieve capabilities, but not as evidence objects. (See Chapter 7).

Option 3, the EDRMS, manages emails which are records as records in a separate system where all of their records characteristics are assured, their retention is managed and they are with other related records created using other systems. (See Chapter 7).

8.3 Scenarios

In order to look at which option might be the most suitable approach for a given context and how it might work in practice, we will explore three different scenarios. For each scenario the following points are considered in order to create a simple checklist of the main requirements in each scenario:

- the role of email, the nature of the emails, the challenges and issues
- the option to be adopted
- what needs to be done, i.e. the implications of the option

The strengths and weaknesses of each option are then compared.

8.3.1 The Department of Long Term Planning

The Department of Long Term Planning (DLTP) is a core central government department whose principal responsibility is to lead and direct the government planning cycle and to document the outcomes of planning activity at the national level. Its key objectives are to:

- establish planning strategy on a five year cycle
- monitor and review strategy implementation
- consult widely with all groups in society to assess impact of planning strategy

DLTP employs 600 staff of whom 400 are based in the capital and 50 each in four regional centres. They currently operate a centralised registry system which relies heavily on paper files, but are moving towards the implementation of an electronic records management system to meet the requirements of e-government. There is, however, an inherent mistrust of IT and a reluctance to accept the wider responsibility for recordkeeping which is required of all staff in the e-environment. They use electronic mail extensively for communication with the regional offices on strategy matters and it has become the communication channel of choice for decision-making.

Role and nature of email, challenges and issues

The majority of the DLTP's emails are records which either:

- document a decision between two or more members of staff/groups, or
- are disseminated for information to staff in other locations.

Whilst use of email for personal purposes is allowed, restrictions are tight and therefore only a small percentage of the total email traffic is not business related. Email records comprise:

- the message per se
- the message and attachment, which is only ever a standard office document such as a word-processed document, spreadsheet or PDF file.

It is vital that, as a government department, DLTP's email records have all the characteristics of good records and remain accessible over time, since some will eventually be retained by The National Archives. They will be subject to freedom of information legislation.

Challenges here are:

- the traditional paper mentality
- user fear of IT, and
- the belief that 'it is not my job'.

Option/strategy chosen

Their chosen strategy for managing email is to use the planned EDRMS. In preparation for that, they are beginning the change management process by raising awareness of email management and helping staff to improve their current practice within the context of the email system itself.

What needs to be done?

There are some immediate priorities but all aspects of recordkeeping need to be addressed. The first steps are listed below and the full checklist covering the whole process appears in Appendix A (Chapter 8 Checklist 2).

Step 1 – Develop an email management policy covering

- appropriate use and monitoring
- recordkeeping – exclude use of email archiving functionality
- roles and responsibilities

Step 2 – Establish a fileplan based on a business classification scheme
Step 3 – Creation and capture

- naming conventions
- metadata (for identification, appraisal and retention)
- dealing with threads and attachments
- by whom, when and where records will be captured
- dealing with drafts and duplicates.

8.3.2 Wilberforce & Treat

Wilberforce & Treat is a multinational management and accountancy consultancy, which employs 10,000 staff across five continents. They have major offices in the UK and US and have recently introduced hot desking into their UK office as a result of a major office move to smaller premises. Their main customers are national and multinational companies for whom they develop management strategies or act as auditors. They operate a system of global teams for these top level functions and they are supported in their work by an electronic document management system.

They rely on email for customer support and use it as the preferred method of business communication to maximise the potential of working across global time zones.

Role and nature of email, challenges and issues

The majority of Wilberforce & Treat's emails support collaborative working and customer support. They are records which either:

- document a decision between two or more members of staff/groups
- are disseminated for information to staff in other locations, or
- support administrative arrangements (e.g. virtual project meetings) and therefore have a relatively short lifetime.

The use of email for personal purposes is allowed and, because of travel and time zones, is well used. Email records comprise:

- the message per se
- the message and attachment, which is only ever a standard office document such as a word processed document, spreadsheet, presentation or PDF file.

Given its sector and stock exchange listings, Wilberforce & Treat must meet the records requirements of the Sarbanes-Oxley Act, other financial and fiscal regulations (as monitored and applied by the Financial Services Authority – FSA) and data protection. However, their prime concern is the here and now and competitive advantage through the sharing of information.

Challenges here are:

- volume and tendency to over-use email (e.g. instead of a conversation)
- separation of personal and business emails,
- identification and capture of email records from the many that are ephemeral/transitory.

Option/strategy chosen

Their chosen strategy for managing email is to use the existing EDMS for emails which are not classed as ephemeral, building in additional retention and security functionality, and to train staff to use the email system itself to manage all other business and personal emails.

What needs to be done?

Again, there are some immediate priorities, but all aspects of recordkeeping need to be addressed. The first steps are listed below and the full checklist covering the whole process appears in Appendix A (Chapter 8 Checklist 2).

Step 1 – Develop an email management policy covering

- appropriate use and monitoring
- recordkeeping – exclude use of email archiving functionality
- roles and responsibilities

Step 2 – Establish guidelines

- when to use email, how to write email, appropriate content
- discovery issues
- managing personal emails within the email system
- managing email records within the EDMS

Step 3 – Capture

- naming conventions
- metadata (for identification, appraisal and retention)
- dealing with threads and attachments
- by whom, when and where will records be captured
- dealing with drafts and duplicates.

8.3.3 MemoraBallia

MemoraBallia is a mail order company dealing in sporting memorabilia for ball games. They were established in 1998 with a staff of four and now have ten employees. The work is divided between three sections which are:

- Marketing and buying
- Sales and financial management
- Packing and despatch

The Managing Director, who created the company, oversees the operations of the three sections and is responsible for business planning.

Since 2002, when they set up a website, they have started to take orders by email as well as by post and by telephone. Email is also used for contacts with suppliers and by the Managing Director to keep in touch with Marketing and Sales sections, but Packing do not use email at all.

Role and nature of email, challenges and issues

MemoraBallia primarily uses email for e-business (i.e. e-ordering) with some limited communications use between the Managing Director and some staff. Emails are therefore records which either:

- document a transaction with a customer, or
- capture a communication/decision.

Use of email for personal purposes is strictly forbidden. Email records comprise:

- the message per se
- the message and attachment, which is only ever a standard office document such as a word-processed document, spreadsheet or PDF file
- the online order.

  Email orders must be retained for audit and tax purposes.

Challenges here are:

- use of email is not universal
- managing same types of records in different formats, e.g. orders.

Option/strategy chosen

Their chosen strategy for managing email is to use the email system itself, in particular individual and shared folders to organise emails, auto deletion and to move email records to a read-only shared directory structure for audit and tax purposes.

What needs to be done?

As with the other two scenarios there are immediate priorities and a comprehensive list of elements to address. The immediate steps are listed below and the full checklist is in Appendix A (Chapter 8 Checklist 2).

Step 1 – Develop an email management policy covering

- appropriate use and monitoring
- recordkeeping – exclude use of email archiving functionality
- roles and responsibilities

Step 2 – Address the following issues

- user space limits
- training

- monitoring use
- business continuity and disaster recovery
- risk management

Step 3 – Establish guidelines

- when to use email, how to write email, appropriate content
- discovery issues
- managing personal emails within the email system.

8.4 Comparison of the options

The management of emails which are records needs to address all of the topics covered in this guide. The majority of organisations do not have an EDRMS or an EDMS but, if they are email users, then they do have the email system. They must therefore use its functionality to support the efficient management of all emails and build in the best controls they can to support the effective management of those deemed to be business records which have more than ephemeral value.

To ensure the successful use of the email or any other system for managing email records, it is crucial to have an email policy. This is clearly evident from the scenarios examined above. The other priorities will be determined by the approach adopted with the policy acting as the foundation. We have highlighted the first steps to be taken in the different scenarios, but it is essential for all scenarios to cover all aspects as listed in the two checklists in Appendix A.

And finally some tips for managing emails which are not records (JISC Electronic Records Management Training Package www.jisc.ac.uk/project_ermpackage.html):

Top ten tips for managing email.

1. When each message is read for the first time, make a decision to save important information to folders then delete the email.
2. Discourage the use of email for sending the content of documents in large attachments. Encourage storing documents for general use in a more reliable place such as a networked drive or an intranet.
3. Train users to clear out their email archives as a matter of routine. If they are stored on the server you can threaten to delete anything more than 3 months old. BUT be sure to warn them in advance and make sure there are instructions available on how to do it.
4. Encourage users to de-register from mail groups they are no longer making use of – why waste time on email messages that are simply clogging up the system?
5. Encourage users to set up an automatic facility to empty messages from the deleted folder when exiting the email system. This command is accessible through *Tools / Options / Maintenance*
6. Encourage email etiquette, which is simply the use of appropriate business-like language which will avoid confusion on the part of the receiver and ensure that the message is received and understood.
7. Always use an appropriate "Subject line" in your message (see best practice for suggestions)
8. Always (re)read the email before you send it
9. Use correct grammar, spelling and punctuation since the email needs to be clear and unambiguous, which is what grammar, spelling and punctuation rules are for.
10. Don't send libellous, obscene, offensive or racist remarks

8.5 Further guidance on managing email

There are many good sources of guidance on developing email policies and guidelines and strategies for managing email. These include:

- ANSI/ARMA 9-2004. (2004). Requirements for managing electronic messages as records. ARMA.
- e-Policy Institute. www.epolicyinstitute.com
- Flynn, N. and Kahn, R. (2003). Email rules. Amacom.
- The National Archives. (2004). Guidelines on developing a policy for managing email. The National Archives.

See the two checklists in Appendix A on managing email in practice. The first will enable you to assess your current approach and the second provides you with a step-by-step guide to checking the key requirements are met.

Chapter 9

Making the case for records management

Having looked at what is involved in managing records in the e-environment, in this final chapter we step back and look at how to make the business case for managing your organisation's records.

9.1 What is a business case?

In many ways making the case for records management, or a particular element of it, is no different from making the case for a new training programme or staff appraisal process, a new piece of equipment or system, a new building or office relocation, outsourcing a service or recruiting additional personnel. The bottom line is - why should your organisation do it? What is the business need?

To answer these two fundamental questions means identifying:

- the business requirements
- the benefits to your organisation
- the associated risks
- how and when it will be done
- how much it will cost, and
- what will change.

The case will need to be presented to management in such a way that they can make an informed decision about the proposal – and preferably approve it. In preparing a business case the aim is "to convince management of the viability of a proposed course of action and to justify the resource commitment required to achieve the desired outcome" *DIRKS Manual, Appendix 9* (National Archives of Australia, 2001). The case may be very wide ranging if the organisation has hitherto paid little attention to managing its records, or it may be specific, focusing on a particular aspect of managing records such as managing email (as in the previous chapter), outsourcing records storage or developing and implementing a business continuity plan.

It may in fact need to be sold to a particular group of people, a specific individual with the relevant authority or to a range of different stakeholders. Understanding who you need to sell it to and what will attract their attention and support is a vital first step in preparing the business case.

9.2 Preparing the business case

Many organisations have their own generic style of business case – if yours does, then use it. Do not present the case for records management in an unfamiliar style – it may add an unnecessary hurdle.

However, even if your organisation does have its own style, there is some excellent published guidance that can be used to help you prepare it. Rather than repeat much of this valuable information, the aim of this chapter is to highlight the key elements of any business case for records management and some of the key sources of help.

There are some essential elements to any business case, viz.:

- the business requirement(s)
- the options and the recommended option
- a cost-benefit analysis
- a risk analysis
- an implementation plan which outlines resources and timescales.

The business requirement is the reason for the project, i.e. the 'problem' that will be solved. That problem must be set within the organisational context and linked to its mission or goals so that the case for addressing it is as strong as possible. For example, the problem may be that a group of staff working on a project are based in multiple locations, including at home and in the field, operating in different time zones and need to share information and co-author documents. They need electronic access to that information 24/7. Arguably, that might just be 'nice to have' and not mission critical. But if it were linked to an organisational goal which wanted to reduce the product development lifecycle and speed up the time to market, for example in the pharmaceutical sector or parts of the retail sector, then solving the problem would support faster project completion and therefore faster product development. It would probably have other benefits too and it is important in stating the business requirement(s) to establish what the outcomes, benefits and impact of solving the problem will be, together with some measures of success.

Within the broad context of managing an organisation's records and developing a strategy to do so, then Best (BIP 0025:1, 2002) provides some useful ideas whilst referring to sector specific scenarios, ISO 15489-1 Section 4 (2001) contains a list of benefits and McLean (2003) illustrates how, in practice, they can be successfully communicated to different stakeholders.

Having established the business requirement or problem, what are the options or alternative solutions for addressing it? These need to be identified and evaluated so that the strengths and weaknesses, pros and cons, of each one can be readily compared. Although not a preferred solution, for obvious reasons, the *do nothing* option should always be included. It provides an opportunity to highlight the dangers or consequences of *not* addressing the problem. Having presented the options the preferred option should be recommended based on the evaluation.

It is possible that there is more than one suitable option, but it is likely that the cost-benefit analysis will reveal the most appropriate one. For each option the cost-benefit analysis compares the estimated costs with the expected benefits and therefore should consider:

- how much it will cost to implement and maintain
- how much it will save ('hard' or tangible benefits) and what the 'soft' benefits will be, for example better customer service
- if it is the most appropriate approach.

There are a number of standard techniques for conducting a cost-benefit analysis, for example, return-on-investment and break-even analysis (for others see Asprey and Middleton, 2003). All options should to be compared but, depending on the nature of the business case and the organisational context, it may be that a detailed cost-benefit analysis is not required for every option, only the recommended option and possibly the next best alternative. The purpose of the cost-benefit analysis is to demonstrate the 'project' is worth doing and the recommended option is the most appropriate.

The risk analysis section of the business case should identify and assess the operational, technical and financial risks associated with the recommended option. This will cover, for example:

- the impact on staff, customers and other projects or services
- the schedule, scope, dependencies and contingencies
- the stability and reliability of the technical solution (if appropriate) particularly if the technology is very new and not well-proven
- the nature of the financial model and the budget available, the risk of exceeding the budget
- the chances of the project succeeding.

Small scale projects may have no risks or minimal risks attached, but the larger and more complex the project the greater the risk. The crucial part of this section of the business case is to have identified what they are and have developed a strategy for minimising them and managing them if they should arise.

The final part of the business case is the implementation plan, which will cover how the project will be managed, what resources are required, including roles and responsibilities, and a high level project plan providing the overall timescale and schedule.

9.3 Presenting the business case

Having prepared the business case, what remains is to 'sell' it to the relevant audience. Success will depend on getting the message across, which means matching the message to the audience and using the appropriate persuasion techniques. If the audience is the board or most senior executives, then the cost-benefit message must be translated into appropriately strategic 'management speak', for instance relating to competitive advantage or empowered employees. The most appropriate method of persuasion will depend on the individual(s) concerned and/or the organisational priorities and culture. For instance, the threat of legislation or damage to reputation may be a more persuasive argument to high profile organisations and those operating in heavily regulated sectors than the one based on uniqueness or leading edge, which would appeal to entrepreneurial, innovative organisations.

Assuming you have prepared a strong case, presented it well and justified it with the necessary authority and confidence to gain approval, then all that remains is to implement it successfully. The techniques of successful project implementation are well documented elsewhere (e.g. PRINCE 2 www.prince2.com/)

Use the final checklist in Appendix A to plan your approach to making the business case for records management. And good luck with managing your organisation's records!

References

ANSI/ARMA 9-2004. (2004). Requirements for managing electronic messages as records. ARMA.

AS4390:1-6. (1996). Records management. Standards Australia.

Asprey, L. and Middleton, M. (2003). Integrative document and content management: strategies for exploiting enterprise knowledge. Idea Group Publishing.

Atherton, J. (1985-86). From life cycle to continuum: some thoughts on the records management-archives relationship. Archivaria, 21, pp. 43–51.

Audit Commission. (2002). Data remember – improving the quality of patient-based information in the NHS.

Bantin, P. (1998). Electronic records management: a review of the work of a decade and a reflection on future directions. www.indiana.edu/~libarch/ER/encycloarticle9.doc

BBC News UK Edition. (2004). Alert could have stopped Huntley. [available at news.bbc.co.uk/1/hi/uk/3533919.stm]

BBC Radio 4. (2005). Today Programme. Business news with Greg Wood 13 December 2005. www.bbc.co.uk/radio4/today/listenagain/ztuesday_20051213.shtml

Bearman, D. and Hedstrom, M. (1993). Reinventing Archives for Electronic Records: Alternative Service Delivery Options, Electronic Records Management Program Strategies, Archives and Museums Informatics Technical Report, No. 18, edited by Margaret Hedstrom. In: Erlandsson, A. (1996). Electronic records management: a literature review. ICA. www.ica.org/

Bennett, R. (1994). What drives records management. Records Management Journal, 4(1), pp. 65-76.

Best, D. (1996). The fourth resource: information and its management. Aslib/Gower.

Best, D. (2002). BIP 0025-1. Effective records management Part 1: A management guide to value of BS ISO 15489-1. BSI.

Biggest email blunders of 2003. www.buys.co.za/casestudies_email_blunders.htm

BIP 0008-1. (2004). Code of practice for legal admissibility and evidential weight of information stored electronically. BSI.

BIP 0009. (2004). Legal admissibility and evidential weight of information stored electronically. Compliance workbook. BSI.

BIP 0025-1. (2002). Effective records management. Part 1: A management guide to the value of BS ISO 15489. BSI.

BIP 0025-2. (2002). Effective records management. Part 2: A guide to the practical implementation of BS ISO 15489. BSI.

BIP 0025-3. (2003). Effective records management. Part 3: Performance management for BS ISO 15489-1. BSI.

BS 5454. (2000). Recommendations for the storage and exhibition of archival documents. BSI.

BS 6498. (2002). Guide to preparation of microfilm and other microforms that may be required as evidence. BSI.

Boulton, C. (2002). Enron: a wake-up call for records management. www.internetnews.com/bus-news/print.php/967071

Brown, A. (2003). Preserving the digital heritage: building a digital archive for UK Government records. Online Information 2003 Proceedings pp. 65–68.

CAMiLEON. (2003). BBC Domesday. www.si.umich.edu/CAMILEON/domesday/domesday.html

Charities Act 1993 (Public General Acts - Elizabeth II). (1993). Chapter 10. The Stationery Office.

Christian, C. (2001). Echoes of Northridge and I.R.A bombings. Law Technology News, October. http://ltn-archive.hotresponse.com/october01/lessons_learned_p25b.html

Civil Evidence Act 1995 (Public General Acts - Elizabeth II). (1995). Chapter 38. The Stationery Office.

Clarke, M. (2003). Speech given at Information Management eXpo May, Dublin.

Companies Act 1989 (Public General Acts - Elizabeth II). (1989). Chapter 40. The Stationery Office.

Control of Substances Hazardous to Health (COSHH) Regulations. (2002). SI 2002/2677. HMSO.

Darlington, J., Finney, A. and Pearce, A. (2003). Domesday Redux: the rescue of the BBC Domesday project videodiscs. Ariadne, 36, July 2003. www.ariadne.ac.uk/issue36/tna/

Data Protection Act 1998 (Public General Acts – Elizabeth II). (1998) Chapter 29. The Stationery Office.

Defra. Environmental Information Regulations 2004 web pages. www.defra.gov.uk/corporate/opengov/eir/index.htm

Department for Constitutional Affairs. (2002). Code of Practice on the Management of Records. Issued under Section 46 of the Freedom of Information Act 2000. www.dca.gov.uk/foi/codesprac.htm

Department of Health. (1999). HSC 1999/053 For the record: managing records in NHS Trusts and Health Authorities. DoH.

Department of Health. (2003). Better informed? Inspection of the management and use of information in social care. CI (2003) 5. www.dh.gov.uk/assetRoot/04/09/43/27/04094327.pdf and accompanying Social Services Inspectorate Checklist www.dh.gov.uk/assetRoot/04/08/43/50/04084350.pdf

Department of Health. (2006). Records Management: NHS Code of Practice. DoH. www.dh.gov.uk/assetRoot/04/11/40/95/04114095.pdf

e-Government Unit. www.cabinetoffice.gov.uk/e-government/index.asp

Electronic Communications Act 2000 (Public General Acts – Elizabeth II). (2000). Chapter 7. The Stationery Office.

Environmental Information Regulations 2004. (2004). Statutory Instrument 2004 No. 3391. The Stationery Office.

European Commission. Website for pharmaceutical legislation. http://pharmacos.eudra.org/F2/review/index.htm

Festa, P. and Bowman, L. (2002). PC sleuths search for Enron's shredded secrets. Cnet 5 February. http://news.zdnet.co.uk/business/0,39020645,2103739,00.htm

Fellowes. (2003). Guide to retention scheduling.

Fifth Resource. (2004). www.fifthresource.com/about.html

Financial Services and Markets Act 2000. (Public General Acts – Elizabeth II). (2000). Chapter 8. The Stationery Office.

Flynn, N. and Kahn, R. (2003). Email rules. Amacom.

Flynn, S. J. A. (2001). Records continuum model in context and its implications for archival practice. Journal of the Society of Archivists, 22(1), pp. 79-93.

Freedom of Information Act 2000. (Public General Acts – Elizabeth II). (2000). Chapter 36. The Stationery Office.

Fuzeau, P. (2005). Records management: two case studies from the French private sector. In: McLeod, J. and Hare, C. (eds). Managing electronic records. Facet.

Gerr, P.A. (2003). Is Your Information Infrastructure Ready for Today's Compliance Environment? Corporate Board member magazine, 21 July. www.boardmember.com/network/index.pl?section=1031&article_id=11612&show=article (needs sign in)

Hamer, A. C. (2004). The ICSA guide to document retention. ICSA.

Hawley Committee. (1995). Information as an asset: checklist and explanatory notes. KPMG.

Hiatt, J. and Creasey, T. (2003) The definition and history of change management. Change Management Tutorial Series. www.change-management.com/tutorial-definition-history.htm

History Data Service. (1999). Digitising history. Chapter 7. Glossary and Bibliography. http://hds.essex.ac.uk/g2gp/digitising_history/sect71.asp

Horsman, P. (1997). Appraisal on wooden shoes – the Netherlands PIVOT project. Janus, 2.

Human Rights Act 1998 (Public General Acts – Elizabeth II). (1998) Chapter 42. The Stationery Office.

ISO 9000. (2000). Quality assurance standards: Parts 1-4. ISO.

ISO 14001. (2004). Environmental management systems – requirements with guidance for use. ISO.

ISO 15489-1. (2001). Information and documentation – records management. Part 1: General. ISO.

ISO 18925. (2002). Imaging materials. Optical disc media: storage practices. ISO.

ISO 19005-1. (2005). Document management – Electronic document file format for long-term preservation – Part 1: Use of PDF 1.4 (PDF/A-1). ISO.

ISO 23081-1. (2006). Information and documentation – records management processes. Part 1: Principles. ISO.

ISO/IEC 17799. (2000). Information technology: Code of practice for information security management. ISO.

ISO/TR 15489-2. (2001). Information and documentation – records management. Part 2: Guidelines. ISO.

JISC Electronic Records Management Training Package. (2004). JISC. www.jisc.ac.uk/project_ermpackage.html

Law Commission. (2001). Electronic commerce: formal requirements in commercial transactions. Advice from the Law Commission. www.lawcom.gov.uk/docs/e-commerce.pdf

Lexmark Inc. (2005). Marketing and advertising worst professions for untidy desks. On Creative Match website www.creativematch.co.uk/viewNews/?90924

Lyman, P. et al. (2003). How much information? 2003. University of California at Berkeley. www.sims.berkeley.edu/research/projects/how-much-info-2003

McDonald, J. (2005). The wild frontier ten years on. In: McLeod, J. and Hare, C. (eds). Managing electronic records. Facet.

McDonald, J. (1995). Managing records in the modern office: taming the wild frontier. Archivaria, 39, pp. 70–79.

McKie, R. and Thorpe, V. (2002). Digital Domesday Book last 15 years not 1000. The Observer, 3 March.

McKinley, T. (1997). Managing all information assets. Document Management Magazine, July/August. www.infologics.com/media2.htm

McLean, B. (2003). The business case for implementing ISO 15489. Records Management Bulletin, 115, pp. 7–12.

MHRA (Medicines and Healthcare products Regulatory Agency). (2005) How we regulate medicines. www.mhra.gov.uk/home/idcplg? IdcService=SS_GET_PAGE&nodeId=27

Minnesota Historical Society. (2002). Trustworthy Information Systems Handbook: Appendix G, Legal Risk Analysis. www.mnhs.org/preserve/records/tis/Legalriskoptions.html

Morelli, J. (1999). Process-driven retention scheduling. Records Management Bulletin, 94, pp. 3-8.

Morelli, J. (2005). Business classification schemes: issues and options. Records Management Bulletin, 124 (Feb 2005), pp. 15, 17–21.

MoReq (Model Requirements for the Management of Electronic Records). (2001). Cornwell. www.cornwell.co.uk/moreq.html

The National Archives. (1998). Records management standards: an introduction.

The National Archives. (1999). Management, appraisal and preservation of electronic records Vol. 1: Principles. www.nationalarchives.gov.uk/ electronicrecords/advice/guidelines.htm

The National Archives. (2001). E-government Policy Framework for Electronic Records Management. www.nationalarchives.gov.uk/ electronicrecords/pdf/egov_framework.pdf

The National Archives. (2002). Functional requirements for Electronic Records Management Systems requirements for electronic records management systems. www.nationalarchives.gov.uk/electronicrecords/ function.htm

The National Archives. (2002) List of approved systems. www. nationalarchives.gov.uk/electronicrecords/reqs2002/approved.htm

The National Archives. (2004). Guidelines on developing a policy for managing email. The National Archives.

The National Archives Model action plans for achieving compliance with the Lord Chancellor's Code of Practice on the management of records. www.nationalarchives.gov.uk/policy/foi/

The National Archives. Retention and disposal schedules. www.national archives.gov.uk/recordsmanagement/advice/schedules.htm

National Archives of Australia. (2003). Keeping electronic records. Managing electronic records: the background. www.naa.gov.au/recordkeeping/er/keeping_er/background.html

National Archives of Australia. (2000). Administrative Functions Disposal Authority. www. naa.gov.au/recordkeeping/disposal/authorities/GDA/afda/summary.html

National Archives of Australia. (2001). DIRKS: A strategic approach to managing business information. (Also known as the DIRKS Manual). www.naa.gov.au/recordkeeping/dirks/dirksman/dirks.html

Office of the e-Envoy. (2000). E-government: a strategic framework for public services in the Information Age. http://archive.cabinetoffice.gov.uk/e-envoy/resources-pdfs/$file/Strategy.pdf

O'Shea, G. (1996). Keeping electronic records: issues and strategies. Provenance, 1 (2), March. www.netpac.com/provenance/vol1/no2/features/erecs1a.htm

Parker, E. (2003). Revised study of the records lifecycle. Function activity model (FAM) and records retention schedule (RRS). JISC. www.jisc.ac.uk/index.cfm?name=srl_structure

PD 0016. (2001). Guide to scanning business documents. BSI.

PD 0017. (2001). Guide to the preparation of business documents. BSI.

PD 5000. (2002). Legal admissibility: an international code of practice for electronic documents and e-business transactions for evidence, audit, long term duty of care. BSI.

Penn, I. A., Pennix, G. B. and Coulson, J. (1994). Records management handbook. 2nd ed. Gower Publishing.

Piggott, M. and McKemmish, S. (eds). (1994). The records continuum: Ian McLean and Australian Archives first fifty years. Sydney.

PRINCE2. (2001). Introduction to PRINCE2 – management overview. www.ogc.gov.uk/prince2/

Public Records Act. 1958 and 1967 (Public General Acts – Elizabeth II). (1967). The Stationery Office.

Reed, B. (2005). Reading the records continuum: interpretations and explorations. Archives & Manuscripts, 33(1), pp. 18–43.

Regulation of Investigatory Powers Act. 2000 (Public General Acts – Elizabeth II). (2000). Chapter 23. The Stationery Office.

Retention Guidelines for Local Authorities. (2003). www.rms-gb.org.uk/resources/91

Robek, M. F., Brown, G. F. and Maedke, W. O. (1987). Information and records management. 3rd ed. Glencoe.

Rogers, L. (2003). Prague: saving the books. Humanities, 24 (2) March/April. www.neh.fed.us/news/humanities/2003-03/prague.html

Rothenberg, J. (2002). Preservation of the times. Information Management Journal, 36 (2) March/April, pp. 38–43.

Rothenberg, J. (1996). Digital preservation summary. Practical experiences in digital preservation. Conference jointly organised by The National Archives and the International Council on Archives 2–4 April 2003, National Archives, Kew.

Rothenberg, J. (1995). Ensuring the longevity of digital documents. Scientific American, 272 (1), January, pp. 42–47.

The Sarbanes-Oxley Act. (2002). Enacted as the Public Company Accounting Reform and Investor Protection Act of 2002. www.ereinsure.com/docs/SOX404eRewhitepaper.pdf

Scottish Information Commissioner. www.itspublicknowledge.info/

Shepherd, E. and Yeo, G. (2003). Managing records: a handbook of principles and practice. Facet Publishing.

SI 2005/2789 2005. Elizabeth II. The medicines for human use (manufacturing, wholesale dealing and miscellaneous amendments) regulations 2005. The Stationery Office.

Slater & Gordon. (2002). Australia's landmark tobacco decision. Media release, 11 April. www.slatergordon.com.au/classactions/docs/MediaRelease11.04.02.pdf

State Records New South Wales. (2004). Disposing of state records. www. records.nsw.gov.au/publicsector/disposal/disposal.htm

State Records New South Wales. (2003). Strategies for document government business: The DIRKS manual. Sydney, Australia. www.records.nsw.gov.au/publicsector/DIRKS/final/title.htm

Stephens, D. O. (2005). The Sarbanes-Oxley Act: records management implications. Records Management Journal, V15(2), pp. 98–103.

Terror in the US. London shocked but prepared. (2001). ComputerWeekly.com, 12 September.

Turnbull Report. (1999). Internal Control: *Guidance for directors on the Combined Code (The Turnbull Report).* Institute of Chartered Accountants.

Upward, F. (2000). Modelling the continuum as paradigm shift in recordkeeping and archiving processes and beyond – a personal reflection. Records Management Journal, 10 (3), pp. 115–139.

Upward, F. (1996). Structuring the records continuum. Part one: post-custodial principles and properties. Archives and Manuscripts, 24 (2), pp. 268-285. Updated version in www.sims.monash.edu.au/research/rcrg/publications/recordscontinuum/fupp1.html

VAT (Value Added Tax) Act 1994 (Public General Acts – Elizabeth II). (1994). Chapter 23. HMSO.

Victoria Electronic Records Strategy (VERS). (2003). www.prov.vic.gov.au/vers/

Wiggins, B. (2002). Effective document management: unlocking corporate knowledge. Gower.

ZyLAB (2002). News Service Listserver@ZyLAB.NL 18 December.

Appendix A: Checklists

Chapter 4 – Managing records for legal and regulatory compliance – Checklist

	Yes	No	Don't know
Admissibility of e-records • digital signatures used • systems documented • systems operated by skilled/trained people	☐ ☐ ☐	☐ ☐ ☐	☐ ☐ ☐
Legal discovery • high risk • medium risk • low risk	☐ ☐ ☐	☐ ☐ ☐	☐ ☐ ☐
Relevant laws, standards and regulations • freedom of information • data protection • human rights • electronic communications • regulation of investigatory powers • e-commerce • environmental information regulations • sector specific legislation • sector specific regulations • national standards • international standards	☐ ☐ ☐ ☐ ☐ ☐ ☐ ☐ ☐ ☐ ☐	☐ ☐ ☐ ☐ ☐ ☐ ☐ ☐ ☐ ☐ ☐	☐ ☐ ☐ ☐ ☐ ☐ ☐ ☐ ☐ ☐ ☐
Sources of help in your organisation • lawyer/legal department • company secretary • heads of functions • records management colleagues	☐ ☐ ☐ ☐	☐ ☐ ☐ ☐	☐ ☐ ☐ ☐

Chapter 5 – Risk Management and business continuity – Checklist

	Yes	No	Don't know
Policy • Risk management • Disaster management and recovery	☐ ☐	☐ ☐	☐ ☐
Documentation • Risk register • Disaster plan	☐ ☐	☐ ☐	☐ ☐
Personnel • Risk champion • Risk assessment team • Disaster champion • Disaster team	☐ ☐ ☐ ☐	☐ ☐ ☐ ☐	☐ ☐ ☐ ☐
Procedures • Monitor and review risk register • Test disaster plan	☐ ☐	☐ ☐	☐ ☐
Resources • Backup systems • Disaster recovery provision	☐ ☐	☐ ☐	☐ ☐
Training • Risk management • Disaster management and recovery	☐ ☐	☐ ☐	☐ ☐

Chapter 6 – Scheduling records for retention – Checklist

	Yes	No	Don't know
Retention/disposal schedule • developed • implemented	☐ ☐	☐ ☐	☐ ☐
Retention schedule format • standalone • metadata in an EDRMS • metadata in a business system(s)	☐ ☐ ☐	☐ ☐ ☐	☐ ☐ ☐
Retention schedule structure • records based • functions based	☐ ☐	☐ ☐	☐ ☐
Retention schedule content and coverage • records descriptions • retention period • reason for retention • core records/functions • common records/functions • legacy records/functions	☐ ☐ ☐ ☐ ☐ ☐	☐ ☐ ☐ ☐ ☐ ☐	☐ ☐ ☐ ☐ ☐ ☐
Official records • electronic version • paper version • official record holder identified	☐ ☐ ☐	☐ ☐ ☐	☐ ☐ ☐
Copies managed	☐	☐	☐
Transitory records identified and managed	☐	☐	☐
Risk management strategy	☐	☐	☐

Chapter 7 – Approaches to managing electronic records – Checklist

	Yes	No	Don't know
Systems for recordkeeping • EDRMS • ERMS • Standard Office Software • Workflow system	☐ ☐ ☐ ☐	☐ ☐ ☐ ☐	☐ ☐ ☐ ☐
Preservation strategy • Emulation • Migration	☐ ☐	☐ ☐	☐ ☐
Storage media • Magnetic • Magneto-optical (CDROM) • Other	☐ ☐ ☐	☐ ☐ ☐	☐ ☐ ☐
Backup strategy	☐	☐	☐
Options • EDRMS for whole or part • Embed records management functionality into business processes • Use standard office software and best practice guidelines	☐ ☐ ☐	☐ ☐ ☐	☐ ☐ ☐
Preparing for change • Designated recordkeeping responsibility • Raising awareness • Skills training • Manuals and other documentation	☐ ☐ ☐ ☐	☐ ☐ ☐ ☐	☐ ☐ ☐ ☐
Effective partnerships • IT + Administration + Recordkeeping	☐	☐	☐

Chapter 8 – Managing email in practice

Checklist 1

	Yes	No	Don't know
Email use • personal use • business use	☐ ☐	☐ ☐	☐ ☐
Risks • low risk of embarrassment • medium risk of embarrassment • high risk of embarrassment • managed	☐ ☐ ☐ ☐	☐ ☐ ☐ ☐	☐ ☐ ☐ ☐
Email policy • acceptable use • recordkeeping	☐ ☐	☐ ☐	☐ ☐
Email guidelines	☐	☐	☐
Options • manage emails within the email system and/or the e-office environment • use an EDMS • use an EDRMS	☐ ☐ ☐	☐ ☐ ☐	☐ ☐ ☐
Management processes • creation • capture • organisation • access and use • retention • 'archiving'	☐ ☐ ☐ ☐ ☐ ☐	☐ ☐ ☐ ☐ ☐ ☐	☐ ☐ ☐ ☐ ☐ ☐
Training	☐	☐	☐
Space restrictions	☐	☐	☐

Checklist 2

Step in process	Requirements	Yes	No	Don't Know
Policy	• appropriate use and monitoring	☐	☐	☐
	• recordkeeping – exclude use of email archiving functionality	☐	☐	☐
	• roles and responsibilities	☐	☐	☐
Guidelines	• when to use email, how to write email, appropriate content	☐	☐	☐
	• discovery issues	☐	☐	☐
	• managing personal emails within the email system	☐	☐	☐
	• managing email records within the EDRMS	☐	☐	☐
Creation	• naming conventions	☐	☐	☐
	• metadata	☐	☐	☐
	• threads and attachments	☐	☐	☐
	• digital signatures	☐	☐	☐
	• encryption	☐	☐	☐
Capture	• who (responsible) and when	☐	☐	☐
	• where – personal/ public shared mailboxes; EDRMS	☐	☐	☐
	• metadata (incl. appraisal, retention)	☐	☐	☐
	• drafts, duplicates	☐	☐	☐

(continued on next page)

Step in process	Requirements	Yes	No	Don't Know
Organisation and use	• directory structures for personal /shared mailboxes	☐	☐	☐
	• EDRMS fileplan (based on business classification scheme)	☐	☐	☐
	• access	☐	☐	☐
Pluralisation (Dissemination/ sharing/ retention)	• disposition/retention – auto delete rules for personal email	☐	☐	☐
	• access	☐	☐	☐
	• preservation	☐	☐	☐
Other issues	• User space limits	☐	☐	☐
	• Training	☐	☐	☐
	• Monitoring	☐	☐	☐
	• business continuity/ disaster recovery	☐	☐	☐
	• risk management	☐	☐	☐

Chapter 9 – Making the case for records management – Checklist

	Yes	No	Don't Know
Business case made	☐	☐	☐
Business case needed	☐	☐	☐
Key stakeholders • senior management/executives • lawyers/company secretary • auditors/quality management • marketing/sales/customer service • IT/systems administrators • production • others	☐☐☐☐☐☐☐	☐☐☐☐☐☐☐	☐☐☐☐☐☐☐
Business case strategy • benefits • threats • risks	☐☐☐	☐☐☐	☐☐☐
Business case format • in-house style • DIRKS style • other style	☐☐☐	☐☐☐	☐☐☐

Appendix B: Glossary of terms

This glossary comprises a list of key definitions. Some of the definitions come from three published glossaries/terms and definitions which provide more comprehensive lists:

1. The InterPARES glossary www.interpares.org/display_file. cfm?doc=ip1_glossary.pdf
2. ISO 15489-1. Information and documentation – records management. Part 1: General. ISO, 2001.
3. Shepherd, E. and Yeo, G. (2003) Managing records: a handbook of principles and practice. Facet Publishing.

Appraisal: the act of assigning value to a record in order to establish retention periods

Authenticity: "the quality of being authentic, or entitled to acceptance. As being authoritative or duly authorized, as being what it professes in origin or authorship, as being genuine." (InterPARES)

Business classification scheme: "Business classification schemes identify, label and define the functions and activities of an organisation. They also map the hierarchical and other relationships between those functions and activities." (National Archives of Australia)

Business continuity: ensuring the ongoing operation of an organisation's business by managing risks

Capture: act of incorporating a record with its metadata into a recordkeeping system

Creation: the first phase of the existence of a record and the point at which its lifetime should be planned based on the importance of the business transaction to which it relates

Disaster recovery: preparation to prevent disasters and, in the event of a disaster, to ensure that business resumes as soon as possible and that full recovery occurs with minimum delay

Disposition: "range of processes associated with implementing records retention, destruction or transfer decisions. . ." (ISO 15489)

Electronic record: "a record that is created (made or received and set aside) in electronic form" (InterPARES)

Emulation: the act of recreating a hardware and software environment so that electronic information from an obsolete system can be accessed from a current system

Fileplan: a tool for grouping (classifying) records and other business information in an organisation, developed from its business classification scheme. Alternatively called a record plan or records classification scheme it supports "the capture, titling, retrieval, maintenance and disposal of records and other corporate information." (National Archives of Australia)

Legacy: collections of paper records or records from systems which are no longer in current use, but where the records still need to be retained.

Metadata: "data describing context, content and structure of records and their management through time" (ISO 15489)

Migration: "act of moving records from one system to another, while maintaining the records' authenticity, integrity, reliability and usability" (ISO 15489)

Official record holder: the named person or section or department whose responsibility it is to ensure the master copy of the record is protected and managed

Preservation: "processes and operations involved in ensuring the technical and intellectual survival of authentic records through time" (ISO 15489)

Record: "information created, received, and maintained as evidence and information by an organisation or person, in pursuance of legal obligations or in the transaction of business (ISO 15489)"

Record series: "a series comprises the records of all of the activities that are instances of a single process. A series may be large or small: it is distinguished, not by size, but by the fact that it provides evidence of a particular process. If an activity take place that is unique, rather than an instance of a process, its records form a series in their own right" (Shepherd and Yeo)

Recordkeeping: "making and maintaining complete, accurate and reliable evidence of business transactions in the form of recorded information. Recordkeeping includes:

- creating records in the course of business activity and the means to ensure the creation of adequate records;
- the design, establishment and operation of recordkeeping systems; and
- managing records used in business (traditionally regarded as the domain of records management) and as archives (traditionally regarded as the domain of archives administration)." (Standards Australia (2002), *Australian Standard for Records Management*, AS ISO 15489)

Records continuum: a model for recordkeeping in the electronic environment comprising the four records management themes of transaction, identity, evidence and recordkeeping and the four processes of creation, capture, use and pluralisation

Records management: "the field of management responsible for the efficient and systematic control of the creation, receipt, maintenance, use and disposition of records, including processes for capturing and maintaining evidence of and information about business activities and transactions in the form of records" (ISO 15489)

Reliability: being able to be trusted because it is a true record of what happened and will retain that characteristic into the future

Risk management: a framework for identifying risks, analysing and assessing their likelihood and impact, and planning strategies to mitigate their effects or recover from disasters if the risks materialise

Retention schedule: a list of the record series in an organisation with requirements for how long they should be kept in the various stages of their life and, in some cases, the justification for the periods specified

Transitory records: records with a relatively short lifespan, e.g. agendas for meetings because they become incorporated into the minutes, or working copies of official records which can be destroyed once their convenience value has been satisfied

Vital records: those records which are essential to the continued operation of an organisation after a disaster

Workflow: the flow of information through a business process, usually now used in relation to automated systems which route transaction records through a business process

Appendix C: Selected further resources

Books

Ellis, J. A. (ed.) (2000). *Selected essays in electronic recordkeeping in Australia.* Australian Society of Archivists.

A collection of 12 chapters, written by records professionals, covering principles and strategies for addressing the challenge of managing electronic records and including a case study.

Kennedy, J. and Schauder, C. (1998). *Records management: a guide to corporate recordkeeping.* 2nd ed. Longman.

A revised edition of the 1994 text to take into account the Australian Standard AS 4390-1996: Records Management and the growing dominance of electronic recordkeeping. A practical and easy to read text providing a very good introduction to the major elements of records management and illustrated with cartoons. Each chapter ends with exercises, although answers are not supplied, and includes further references.

McLeod, J. and Hare, C. (eds). (2005). *Managing electronic records.* Facet Publishing.

A collection of views, experiences and expertise from a range of international records management experts from the public and private sectors, on the theory and practice of managing electronic records as business and information assets. Explores issues and solutions for the range of key stakeholders in records management.

Sampson, K. L. (2002). *Value-added records management: protecting corporate assets, reducing business risks.* Greenwood Press. 2002.

A practical guide which underlines the importance of records for business effectiveness and efficiency and the need to protect them by minimising risks and maximising their value.

Shepherd, E. and Yeo, G. (2003). *Managing records: a handbook of principles and practice.* Facet Publishing.

A thorough and detailed review of theory and practice of records management. Excellent list of publications, professional associations and other sources of information.

Journals

Informaa Quarterly

The official journal of the Records Management Association of Australasia. Subscription enquiries to Records Management Association of Australasia.

Email: admin@rmaa.com.au
Web: www.rmaa.com.au

Information Management & Technology

A journal covering the latest developments in records, document and information management. Subscription enquiries to CimTech Ltd Innovation Centre, University of Hertfordshire, College Lane, Hatfield, AL10 9AB, UK.

E-mail: c.cimtech@herts.ac.uk
Web: www.cimtech.co.uk

Records Management Bulletin

The journal of the UK Records Management Society containing articles from practitioners and news of forthcoming events. The bulletin is free to members of the Records Management Society.

Email: info@rms-gb.org.uk
Web: www.rms-gb.org.uk/

Records Management Journal

A journal publishing material on current research and practice, featuring a themed international issue and including reviews of recent publications. Subscription enquiries to Emerald Group Publishing Limited, 60/62 Toller Lane, Bradford, BD8 9BY, UK.

E-mail: subscriptions@emeraldinsight.com

Web: www.emeraldinsight.com/info/journals/rmj/rmj.jsp

Information Management Journal

The journal of the Association of Records Managers and Administrators Inc. Subscription enquiries to ARMA International.

Web: www.arma.org/imj/index.cfm

Journal of the Society of Archivists and *ARC Newsletter*

The monthly ARC Newsletter contains reports on matters of professional importance, sections on records management, conservation, education and training and other topics, as well as a diary of events. The journal covers professional issues in greater depth and includes reviews of recent publications. Both publications are free to members of the Society. Contact Society of Archivists.

Email: societyofarchivists@archives.org.uk

Web: www.archives.org.uk

Listservs (List Servers)

ARCHIVES-NRA – Archives, conservators and records managers.

To subscribe, go to http://www.jiscmail.ac.uk/lists/ARCHIVES-NRA.html

ERECS-L – Management and preservation of electronic records.

LISTSERV@LISTSERV.ALBANY.EDU. To subscribe, see details at ARMA website http://www.arma.org/erecords/listserv.cfm

RECORDS-MANAGEMENT-UK – Records management. To subscribe, go to http://www.jiscmail.ac.uk/lists/RECORDS-MANAGEMENT-UK.html

Professional associations

AIIM Europe

The IT Centre, 8 Canalside, Lowesmoor Wharf, Worcester, WR1 2RR, UK.
  Email:info@aiim.org.uk
  Web: www.aiim.org.uk

Association of Records Managers and Administrators (ARMA International)

13725 W. 109th Street, Suite 101, Lenexa, KS 66215, USA
  Email: hq@arma.org
  Web: www.arma.org

CILIP (Chartered Institute of Library and Information Professionals)

7 Ridgmount Street, London WC1E 7AE, UK.
  Email: info@cilip.org.uk
  Web address: www.cilip.org.uk

CimTech Ltd

Innovation Centre, University of Hertfordshire, College Lane, Hatfield, AL10 9AB, UK.
  E-mail: c.cimtech@herts.ac.uk
  Web: www.cimtech.co.uk

Records Management Association of Australia

GPO Box 1059, Brisbane, Queensland 4001, Australia.
Email: admin@rmaa.com.au
Web: www.rmaa.com.au

Records Management Society of Great Britain

Woodside, Coleheath Bottom, Speen, Princes Risborough,
Buckinghamshire, HP27 0SZ, UK.
Email: info@rms-gb.org.uk
Web: www.rms-gb.org.uk/

Society of Archivists

Prioryfield House, 20 Canon Street, Taunton, Somerset, TA1
1SW, UK.
Email: societyofarchivists@archives.org.uk
Web: www.archives.org.uk

NB The continued existence of these Internet addresses cannot be guaranteed by the authors.

Index

Note: page numbers in *italics* denote references to Figures/ Tables.